KEYS TO
DEALING
WITH
BULLIES

Barry E. McNamara, Ed.D.
and
Francine J. McNamara, M.S.W., C.S.W.

BARRON'S

Cover photo © 1997 PhotoDisc, Inc.

DEDICATION

In loving memory of Max Abrams. He touched many lives with love.

All inquiries should be addressed to:
Barron's Educational Series, Inc.
250 Wireless Boulevard
Hauppauge, New York 11788

Library of Congress Catalog Card No. 97-362

International Standard Book No. 0-7641-0163-3

Library of Congress Cataloging-in-Publication Data
McNamara, Barry E., 1949–
     Keys to dealing with bullies / Barry E. McNamara and
Francine J. McNamara.
        p.   cm. — (Barron's parenting keys)
     Includes bibliographical references and index.
     ISBN 0-7641-0163-3
     1. Bullying. 2. School psychology. 3. Parenting.
I. McNamara, Francine. II. Title. III. Series.
    BF637.B85M33   1997
    371.5′8—dc21   97-362
                                      CIP

PRINTED IN THE UNITED STATES OF AMERICA
987654321

CONTENTS

INTRODUCTION

Bullying is not a new phenomenon. What has changed is that it is finally receiving increased attention in professional journals and books, as well as in popular magazines and newspapers. Yet the amount of information available to parents and schools is relatively small considering the fact that 15 percent of the school-age population is directly involved with bullying, either as a bully or a victim. Beyond this 15 percent are the unknown number of students whose lives are affected because they fear they will be the next victim of a bully.

Keys to Dealing with Bullies provides parents with an appreciation of the nature and scope of the problem and with specific solutions, whether you are the parent of a bully or of a victim. The book is divided into six parts. Part One provides an overview of bullying. Parts Two and Three discuss victims and bullies, respectively. Part Four provides parents of victims with ways to help their children, and Part Five provides parents of bullies with ways to help their children. Finally, Part Six deals with schools and what parents can do to get schools involved in this important issue.

One of the most effective deterrents to bullying is adult intervention. This book provides information for parents so they can intervene, employing effective techniques based on the most recent research.

Acknowledgments

A few years ago, a Special Education Parent Teacher Association (SEPTA) asked us to speak on the topic of bullies. Many of their children were victims of bullies in school and no one was doing anything about it. That sparked our interest in a topic that we always felt needed to be addressed in a systematic manner by parents and school personnel. For the many parents who shared their stories of their children's problems dealing with bullies, we are appreciative. During our research for this book, Ellen Bloom, reference librarian at the East Rockaway (NY) Library, was extremely helpful. We thank her for all her assistance in obtaining information on this topic. Grace Freedson, acquisitions editor at Barron's, was open to our proposal and very supportive of the project, and Linda Turner, our editor for *Keys to Parenting a Child with Attention Deficit Disorder* and *Keys to Parenting a Child with a Learning Disability*, has brought the same level of professionalism to this work. We thank both of them. Finally, we'd like to acknowledge our daughters, Tracy and Melissa, for all that makes them so special.

Part One

~~~~~~

BULLYING:
AN OVERVIEW

What is bullying? The term is used very loosely. This section will define the problem and describe characteristics of bullies and their victims and what parents can do. It will also discuss the role of the school in this serious issue.

1

WHAT IS BULLYING?

B ully! Even the word conjures up uncomfortable feelings in adults today who were victims of classroom or
playground teasing, ignoring, or put-downs. What may
have been considered benign name-calling in years past continues to manifest itself in painful ways—from verbal teasing
to acts of physical aggression. It is not something to be minimized. The National Association of School Psychologists
reports that one in seven U.S. schoolchildren is either a bully
or a bullying victim. Moreover, some studies suggest that
these victims feel that adults do little to reduce these incidents. The topic of bullying is clearly an important priority
for parents to explore, whether one or more of their children
is the victim or the bully, or whether one's children are tod-
dlers or teenagers . . . or somewhere in between.

Bullies try to exercise control over their peers by verbally or physically assaulting them. They may be angry,
afraid, hurt, or frustrated themselves, but unable to deal with
these feelings, or they may have learned these behaviors
from significant role models. For them, the outlet is to verbally and/or physically pick on others. Unfortunately, bullies
seem able to select their victims with great precision. They
most often prey on children and adolescents who are unpop-
ular and vulnerable.

The consequences of being bullied can even be fatal. In
one case that was highly publicized, a seventh-grade boy

fatally shot himself because he was tired of being called "fatty" and "a walking dictionary." He shot one of his classmates to death right before he killed himself. Reportedly, his classmates said, "He was just someone to pick on."

Too often, bullying is dismissed as an expected rite of childhood. Children who are teased are often told to "ignore it," but it's not that simple. Bullying can take a terrible toll on the lives of schoolchildren. The fear, the anxiety, and the social isolation suffered by the victims of bullying can result in loss of productivity in school and unknown psychological distress.

Additionally, some researchers feel that victims have lower self-esteem than bullies themselves. For these students, school is no longer a safe haven. Rather, they are fearful playing on the playground and going to and from classes. Even mild forms of verbal abuse have resulted in absences from school, lower grades, and overall anxiety. On top of the short- and long-term psychological damage caused by the actual bullying experienced by these children and adolescents is the damage caused by the failure of parents and school personnel to intervene when they witness bullying behavior.

The purpose of this book is to provide parents with information that will help them become aware of the serious nature of the problem, and more important, with ways to deal with the problem. And, because schools are the place where most bullying occurs, this book includes ways parents can encourage their school district to start programs that address this problem.

2

~~~~~~

WHO ARE
THE BULLIES?

Bullies want to dominate others. They want to control them. They attempt to do this in a number of ways. They may engage in a number of aggressive behaviors from verbally taunting other children, calling them names, and spreading vicious rumors among their classmates, to threatening other children, sometimes even carrying out such threats. Bullies will often engage in physical aggression toward others and may steal money and valuable items from their victims. The act of bullying is characterized by the persistence of these pernicious attacks—they are frequent and ongoing.

Bullies are very good at selecting those students who are likely victims. If the bully is wrong, he can merely select another victim. Ultimately, some victims will give in to the demands of the bully, thereby reinforcing this socially unacceptable behavior. Bullies learn rapidly that aggression works for them.

Who are these bullies? What type of child would willingly inflict harm on others? The research findings are not entirely clear. Many researchers feel that bullies engage in this behavior because it makes them feel important. They may be insecure people who need to make themselves feel resolution. The low self-esteem, fear, and anxiety are reinforced so frequently that the pattern is difficult to break. Over time, victims begin to believe that they deserve this mistreatment. They lack the skills necessary to combat the problem and can become hopeless and even suicidal. The long-term psychological effects of being bullied can be devastating.

4

WHAT CAN
PARENTS DO?

All experts agree that the single most important deterrent to bullying is adult authority. That is, both in the home and in school, adults need to recognize the severity of the problem and do something about it. Bullying is not something to be minimized. Children who are victims of bullies frequently report that when they tell their parents that they are bullied, their parents don't respond. At best, some parents will tell their child to "ignore it"; at worst, they will tell them to "hit them back." Both words of advice are ineffective. Ignoring the inappropriate behavior of your peers is a very effective technique for many behaviors. However, for bullying it doesn't work.

The victim needs a variety of ways to deal with the bully. Research has shown that many victims are very sensitive children who are very troubled by the taunts of bullies and find it difficult, if not impossible, to ignore. Also, bullying frequently involves physical confrontation and children should be able to feel safe and not just ignore physical abuse. We seem to have very different rules of behavior for children and adults. No one would suggest that an adult who is constantly being hit by a fellow worker merely walk away and ignore it, but we often give children that advice. Ignoring, with no other intervention, is not an effective deterrent to bullies.

"Hit them back" may be the worst advice of all that parents can give to their children. As previously noted, victims of bullies tend to be weaker than bullies, physically, socially, emotionally, or intellectually. If these smaller and weaker children try to fight back physically, they will probably lose and encourage the bully to pick on them more frequently. Bullies are very good at selecting their victims. If they are able to inflict physical harm and they continue to "beat up" the victims, the behavior will be reinforced and continue. This is a difficult thing for many parents to accept. They believe it works. Although standing up to the bully may be effective in some situations, hitting back never works. Victims need to be taught to engage in effective interventions to reduce the incidence of bullying, but ignoring it or fighting back doesn't work.

Parents must be positive role models for their children. If children see their parents using force and aggression to get the things they want, they are likely to do the same thing. One of the most obvious things parents can do is to resolve conflicts in the home without physical confrontation. Hitting, spanking, call it what you want, merely shows children that someone bigger and stronger can inflict physical harm. Children who are hit by their parents are more likely to find someone smaller and weaker than them to hit.

Parents should avoid the use of verbally abusive language and sarcasm toward their children. Parents who chastise, name-call, and use derogatory terms toward their children will most likely have children that do the same.

Parents need to reinforce caring and sensitivity toward others. When children display "caring" behavior, parents should praise them. When children are sensitive to the feelings

11

and needs of others, parents should let their children know how pleased they are by this behavior.

When parents model appropriate behaviors, avoid verbally and physically abusive behaviors toward their children, and reinforce appropriate social behaviors, there is a good chance that their children will treat others with kindness. (Subsequent Keys provide specific strategies for parents of bullies and parents of victims.)

Parents need to be positive toward their children. Parents should provide their children with positive reinforcement when they demonstrate an understanding of others' feelings. They should reinforce sensitivity and caring toward others and teach and reinforce appropriate responses to conflict. Parents of bullies and parents of victims can do a great deal to reduce bullying at home and in school. Although there is research evidence to support it, it is insufficient to simply make the statement that bullies are made not born. Most parents do not want their children to be bullies, even if they are doing things that would encourage that type of behavior. Parents can learn to change their behavior in order to change their children's behavior. And clearly no parents want their child to be victimized. These parents also need to learn effective strategies to help their children deal with bullies. However, without the support of the schools, little will be accomplished. Schools are fertile grounds for bullying. In unstructured settings, in lunchrooms, during recess, in isolated hallways, and, unfortunately, in classrooms, many children are fearful of being victimized by a bully.

5

BULLYING AND SCHOOLS

It is impossible to discuss the topic of bullying without discussing schools. The majority of bullying incidents occur going to, coming from, or during school. The primary focus of this book is for parents. However, parents need to be advocates for their children and work with their schools. In order to do this, they need information. Information is power. Parents need to approach school personnel with information that will translate into school programs that address the issue of bullying.

There are not many school-related problems that involve 15 percent of the students that would not receive a great deal of financial and emotional support. In Norway, Japan, and the United Kingdom, there appears to be a great deal more interest in the effects of bullying in the schools. In fact, one textbook for England provides specific suggestions for the areas in and around the school where bullying will more likely occur and ways to deter such incidents by landscaping, playground areas, and so on.

Some experts in the field have suggested that in the United States, violent behavior is tolerated to a higher degree and "standing up" for oneself is a valued attribute in our culture. Schools need to develop clear-cut rules for appropriate

13

behavior and consistent consequence for inappropriate behavior. A school-wide program is the most effective way for schools to deal with bullying. All students must realize that bullying will not be tolerated and all victims must know that they can turn to school personnel for support.

In the case of Michael, mentioned in Key 3, the school social worker intervened. She met with him to empower the third-grader and provide him with techniques he could use when confronting the bully. She also made it clear to him that he does not have to deal with this himself and he should seek out the adult in charge. As is often the case, the bullying occurred in isolated sections of the playground, so the school provided additional supervision during lunchtime. And most important, the school developed a training program for the staff so they could become more aware of the problem and find effective ways to deal with it.

Everyone who works in the school—cafeteria workers, recess monitors, the custodial staff, secretaries, teachers, aides, and administrators—needs to become aware of the severity of the problem. Only then can a comprehensive program be developed.

The program must also include those students with special educational needs. It appears that a disproportionate number of victims of bullies are students who are classified as learning disabled, as well as students diagnosed with attention deficit disorder and those classified as mentally retarded. This, coupled with an increase in the number of students with special education needs being educated in regular classrooms, necessitates their inclusion in any program that addresses bullying in schools.

Finally, parent cooperation and participation is critical. This is true for all school programs. Parents need to understand the nature of the program and to provide interventions at home that are consistent with the goals of the program.

Bullying is not merely a school problem. It is a societal problem that occurs most often in a school setting. A district-wide program that is developed in a cooperative fashion by parents and school personnel will have the best chance of succeeding.

Part Two

VICTIMS

It is critical to identify those children who are victims of bullies. The following Keys will discuss ways to do this as well as the types of victims, their families, gender differences, and the long-term effects of victimization.

One teacher recalled receiving harassing phone calls at least twice per week when she was an eighth-grade student. These were more than silly, annoying phone calls. Many of them were explicitly sexual, making vulgar comments about her and her family. Initially, nothing was done and she was told to hang up the phone immediately. As this dragged on for months, however, her parents decided to report the calls to the police. Eventually, the caller (a classmate) was found, but little was done to address the problem. The caller's parents minimized it, and the victim's parents were just happy that it stopped.

As in the case with boys, where teachers and parents will discuss bullying by boys with the phrase "boys will be boys," it is not unusual to hear "girls can be so vicious." Both statements are sexist and miss the point. The patterns of bullying may be different, but the effect remains the same. It's not a matter of which tactics are "more vicious" (whatever that means!) than others. It is rather simple. Children should feel safe at home and at school. Anything that interferes with that needs to be addressed. Labeling the tactics and interpreting the nature of the tactics prevents swift intervention.

Perhaps the most important aspect of looking at patterns is to recognize that bullying is widespread and there are *many* ways in which a bully can victimize a child. There needs to be movement away from the classic bully to becoming aware of more subtle ways in which children are victimized, regardless of their gender.

10

WHEN VICTIMS GROW UP

What happens to children who are bullied throughout their school years? Intuitively, there is a sense that it must have an impact on their lives in some negative way. It is astounding how adults have such vivid recollections of the times they were bullied. They remember that bully's name, the specific incident, and how it was handled (or not handled) with great precision. Obviously, it had an impact on them. The professional literature does not shed much light on this subject in terms of empirical research; that is, it has not been studied sufficiently to come to sound conclusions. Some researchers have found male victims to be more depressed and have lower self-esteem. Others have suggested that victims (male and female) may be more timid and shy and avoid confrontation at all cost. It has been suggested that this pattern of behavior is then passed on to their children and that they may overreact to perceived instances of bullying, when they are actually normal developmental behaviors.

Victims tend to miss a great deal of school because they are fearful of bullies. Their academic achievement levels tend to be lower than their peers. And although the long-term effect of this has not been studied, it appears feasible to suggest that most victims would not meet their academic potential. This is compounded for those victims with special educational needs.

Some victims don't grow up. That is, some victims feel so overwhelmed by the taunts of their classmates that they see no other option than suicide. In fact, many anti-bullying programs were developed after children committed suicide as a consequence of severe bullying and harassment by their peers.

Part Three

BULLIES

It is important to understand why bullies act the way they do and the kinds of tactics they employ. This section also deals with types of bullies, their families, gender differences, and the long-term effects of being a bully.

11

^^^

BULLIES ARE MADE, NOT BORN

A group of children on a school bus call one child names everyday. If they don't comment on his clothes, they make fun of his physical appearance, his school performance, or his family. This has gone on for months with no intervention from the school. One day, the father of one of the "bullies" was waiting at the bus stop when the driver told him that his son was taunting a "special education child" every day. His father promptly asked his son if he did it; his son replied, "yes," and his father proceeded to slap him in the face at least three times.

A group of Little Leaguers are playing a game on a pleasant sunny day in any particular neighborhood. A seven year old slides into second base and knocks the second-base player down, who gets hurt. Everybody is concerned and fortunately the child is not seriously hurt. On the way home, a mom looks at her son and says, "Great slide Robert; way to be aggressive out there!"

The principal called home today to tell Matthew's parents that he was involved in a fight. He appeared to start it and hurt the kid so hard that his nose bled. After dinner,

Mom, Dad, and Matthew discussed the incident and all agreed he would try to avoid these confrontations in the future. And as they were getting up from the table, the father, with a wink and a nod, said, "Guess you got a good shot in there."

You are in line in a grocery store and a toddler keeps grabbing the candy by the register and the parent says, "Don't touch that." He continues, and finally she slaps his hand and the toddler cries. The parent gets more annoyed and tells him to stop crying. He continues. She takes him out of the food cart, holds him in her arm, and spanks the child, who continues to cry.

Two children are playing with a toy. A third child comes over and takes the toy away. Parents enter the scene. One parent tells her child, "Don't let him do that. Go over there and take it away from him." The child doesn't respond. Now the parent gets even more annoyed. "You have to stick up for yourself. Go over there and get your toy back." The child doesn't move, cries, and the parent looks defeated.

The examples cited above are just a few in which it is clear that a message is being sent to a child: Might equals right. Aggression is valued. If you are bigger and stronger than someone, you can use physical force. It is clear from the professional literature on bullies that this type of parental interaction, over time, can cause children to become bullies.

There is a difference in stating that "bullies are made, not born" rather than "it's their parents' fault." In the former statement, there is no attempt to blame parents. What is necessary is that parents of bullies recognize the powerful impact of their behavior on their children. When they act in an aggressive manner, their children will follow. When they reward aggression, their children will display this behavior. And when they use verbal abuse and physical aggression toward their children, their children will find someone smaller and weaker than they to do the same. This is not a predisposed condition; rather, these are learned behaviors. There may be some small evidence that temperamental differences can also influence bullying, but the overwhelming findings from the research is that parents play the major role. Some children might also be influenced by the type of movies, TV, games, and books they are exposed to. However, this is also related to family characteristics—bullies tend not to have too much structure in their lives, and their parents are not as involved as parents of children who are not bullies.

The first step for parents of bullies is to recognize that this generation link has to be broken. In order for their child to act in some socially acceptable ways, parents need to change their own patterns. This is not as easy as it appears. Some of the examples given in the beginning of the Key might not be perceived as a "problem" for a lot of parents. A lot of parents feel strongly about "standing up for oneself," being aggressive, or "being in charge." These are viewed as valuable attributes. And it's not their fault that they feel this way. Society appears to be somewhat ambivalent regarding these traits. The overly aggressive person, whether it be in sports, politics, or business, is often held in high regard by many.

Specific recommendations are made in subsequent Keys for some very effective parenting techniques that can help parents of bullies break this cycle and provide children with models of kindness and caring to others.

12

~~~~~~

TYPES OF BULLIES

M ost bullies are aggressive and like to be in charge, at all costs. They also tend to lack empathy and guilt. This fits the stereotypic image of a bully—a physically aggressive person who threatens or injures others.

Bullies engage in a wide range of antisocial and/or aggressive behaviors that range from mild, such as pushing or shoving another child, to threatening someone with a weapon. In addition to these acts of physical aggression, they many engage in acts of social alienation, such as gossiping to maliciously excluding someone from the group. Bullies are also verbally aggressive and may engage in occasional name-calling and taunting to verbal threats of violence. Finally, bullies may attempt to intimidate others by threatening to reveal personal information forcing victims to engage in illegal acts or threatening with a weapon. Regardless of the act, the object is the same: to exert power over another individual.

Many people would like to believe that below this exterior is an insecure person with low self-esteem. This is not always the case. A number of experts suggest that bullies have unusually little anxiety and insecurity and do not have low self-esteem.

Bullies are very different from most children. They tend to interpret others' behaviors as being hostile, even if this is not so. For example, a mild brush against them in a hall may be perceived as a physically aggressive act. If you are always looking for trouble, you'll probably find it. Researchers suggest that bullies process social information incorrectly—everything is seen as an act of aggression. This in turn, leads to the justification of their own aggressive behavior.

Some bullies may also be victims. Provocative victims, frequently students with attention deficit disorder (ADD), tend to be ineffective in their aggressive behavior. They may say or do something to annoy someone. They get upset rapidly, becoming oppositional and defiant, but they can't sustain this level of aggression and give up. Most often, these children are victims, but at times, because of the nature of their disorder, they may engage in bullying behavior.

Gail was frequently called names because she attended a special class for students with special educational needs. Gail has been classified as learning disabled and she also has the diagnosis of ADD. She hated going to school and frequently complained of stomachaches and headaches. When she was in school, she was usually in the nurse's office. At times, she would "fight back" by being verbally abusive to the students who teased her. However, she was no match for these children. She misunderstood nonverbal cues and always thought these children were talking about her. Whenever she tried to stop it, her "techniques" were ineffective.

One of the hallmarks of bullying is the frequency of the negative behavior—it happens often. There will always be conflicts that children must resolve, ranging from sharing toys to issues over what is fair and what is unfair. Some parents may misinterpret some behaviors their child engages in and automatically think it's bullying. For example, when a four year old resorts to name-calling and/or a child attempts to hurt another's feelings there is reason for concern, but it may not be bullying.

13

FAMILIES OF BULLIES

What roles do parents play in the behavior of a bully? What about other family members? Children learn from observing the behaviors of others, parents being the most obvious role models. If the parent use aggression, it's likely that their children will attempt the same type of aggressive behavior. Parents who use sarcasm and name-calling and belittle their children run the risk that their children will do this to others. And, parents who use spanking and other forms of corporal punishment are sending a clear message to their children that if you are bigger and stronger than someone, you can use physical force against them. There is a strong relationship between parents of bullies and bullies themselves. Parents can change their behaviors, but first they must be aware of them. The purpose of this Key is to identify those factors that contribute to bullying. Parents of bullies obviously learned their behaviors, their coping strategies, and their parenting techniques.

In families of bullies, there appears to be a lack of structure. Children are often allowed to engage in a variety of behaviors under minimal adult supervision. This enables these children to act in an aggressive manner without parental input about their inappropriate behaviors. Over time, their behaviors become part of their social repertoire and become difficult to change.

In these families, communication between parent and child is very authoritarian, if not dictatorial. Parents see their

questionnaire to look at bullying in their school. Once armed with the results, she was able to approach the principal and show him that it is a problem. The school is now in the throes of developing an effective anti-bullying program. According to information presented in the professional literature, this is a problem for all schools, and if the administration is not aware of it, it is even more of a problem. The sooner we address bullying with the seriousness it deserves, the sooner children can attend school in a more safe, caring, and kind environment.

15

WHEN BULLIES GROW UP

It is not unusual for a parent to tell his or her child who is being victimized by a bully: "Don't worry, they'll get theirs in the end." And they may be right. In the long run, the bully does suffer a great deal, as many continue to engage in their tactics throughout their lives. Because they are rewarded for their physical aggressiveness and continue to use this as a way to exert power and get what they want, bullies tend to get involved in the criminal justice system at an early age. They may engage in acts of vandalism and they tend to get involved with drugs and alcohol and other anti-social behaviors. As they move through the adult years, they are five times as likely to have a criminal record than children who were not childhood bullies.

This should not come as a surprise. Bullies tend to lack the social skills necessary to deal with conflicts. As they grow up, they come into situations they cannot deal with; therefore, they act in inappropriate ways. As time goes on, their school performance decreases and they get involved with marginal groups within society. Research also reports that childhood bullies are more likely to be spousal abusers and become parents who are aggressive and abusive to their children.

In simple dollars and cents, bullies cost society a great deal of money. When they are in school, they receive a great deal of services from counseling to tutoring to alternative schools, with most of it being ineffective. They tend to be underdeveloped in their academic and professional lives, pay less taxes, and have shorter, less productive lives, and they tend to use social welfare services.

Part Four

WHAT YOU CAN DO IF YOUR CHILD IS A VICTIM

These Keys provide specific strategies that parents can use if their child is a victim. They provide parents with suggestions for being appropriate role models, the use of reinforcements and punishments, and knowing when to seek professional help.

16

EARLY IDENTIFICATION AND INTERVENTION

The key to resolving any problem is early identification. It is critical to be aware of these indications at an early age. It is known that victims tend to be weaker than their peers who are bullies. These children also tend to be somewhat shy and less aggressive. Parents need to be aware of these characteristics because their child may be "at risk" for being bullied.

Children with special educational needs, in particular those who have been diagnosed as Attention Deficit Hyperactivity Disorder (ADHD) and/or classified as Learning Disabled (LD) are overrepresented as victims. Parents of these children need to be aware that their child may be more likely to become a victim.

Some children who are victims lack age-appropriate social skills. Once again, if you notice that your child has a difficult time getting along with others, doesn't appear to understand "the rules" of social interaction, or doesn't always "get it," then be aware. He may be at risk for being a victim.

There are some warning signs that parents can look for:
• Missing belongings
• Not eating lunch

- Torn clothing
- Unexplained bruises
- Illness
- Temper outbursts
- School problems
- Fear of going to school
- Cutting classes
- Isolation/staying in room
- Few or no friends
- Never/infrequently being invited to parties
- Avoiding school activities, especially lunch/recess

The school nurse is an excellent source of information about the bully/victim problem. Children who are victimized in school make frequent visits to the school nurse. They may do this to avoid activities, especially during unstructured times of the day (lunch/recess/dismissal) or they may go there because of illness or perceived illnesses. There is an association between victimization and common health problems in young children. Children who were being bullied reported not sleeping well, had headaches, and stomachaches, felt sad, and wet their beds. Given this information, it would be wise to consult with the school nurse and not merely discuss the situation as a case of "trying to get out of things."

Parents need to be vigilant for these incidents of victimization. Being involved and interested in your child's school life is important. Being aware of your child's friends and activities will allow you to be more observant if a problem should arise. Ongoing, natural communication with your child will open up dialogue if bullying is occurring. This must go beyond merely asking "How was school today?" to an environment where children feel comfortable and reinforced for sharing their lives with their parents.

18

MORE SUGGESTIONS FOR DEALING WITH A BULLY

Parents of victims need to provide positive experiences for their children. They should be provided with opportunities that enable them to feel good about themselves and to have others see them in a competent way. Below are a few recommendations that will provide your children with positive feedback. They will begin to start seeing themselves in ways other than merely as a victim.

Know Your Child's Strengths and Weaknesses

Speak to your child's teacher to find out exactly what things your child does well and what areas are of concern. The teacher should provide you with his or her opinion about specific activities. It is not unreasonable to solicit advice on these concerns, but remember that it is advice, an opinion.

Thomas, a fourth-grader, was never interested in sports. Unfortunately, this made him a scapegoat in gym class and during recess. When he was picked to be on a team, he was always picked last. And his classmates continuously made fun of his lack of interest and ability. His math teacher shared the fact that Thomas loved statistics.

The teacher talked to the physical education teacher (who was also the baseball coach) and asked if he needed a statistician. Thomas began to work with the coach to perform a much needed job. Students started seeing him as a valued member of "the team" and began to recognize his strengths.

Select Activities that Focus on Strengths

You may think that by selecting activities in an area of weakness, you can encourage your child to improve certain skills. For example, you place your child, who has difficulty with fine motor control, in an origami program, thinking that the practice she gets will improve her fine motor control. On the contrary, the experience will probably be so negative that it will only reinforce her feelings of incompetence in this area. Activities outside of school should be enjoyable and positive and provide opportunities to succeed, not fail.

Select Small Groups or Individualized Activities

Rather than having your child attend a large ice skating class, try a few individual or small group lessons. The cost is not much different than a large class and any initial success will give him the confidence he needs to continue to pursue the activity. Small groups and individualized activities reduce competition and comparisons. Your child will only have to do his best and not worry about how others are doing and how he stacks up against them.

Encourage Special Interests and Hobbies

Few things excite children more than being an expert in a particular area. Having a special interest or hobby allows children to learn more about a subject than most children or adults. There are children who are experts on origami, rocks, gymnastics, snakes, race cars, baseball cards, and on and on. Adults have to ask *them* for information on these subjects. When these children show confidence in a special area of knowledge like this, their competence will spill over into their school life, where the teacher can reinforce this interest.

Interests and hobbies don't just emerge. They are fostered by parents who give their children information through books, magazines, tapes, and discussions, and through taking them on trips to parks, zoos, museums, and other places of interest. A child who visited a Civil War battlefield became incredibly interested in the Civil War and started to listen to tapes, view programs, and eventually read about it. He now knows more about it than most adults! He is proud to have a reputation for this in his school, where teachers sometimes seek him out with questions.

Reinforce Effort

Sometimes children enjoy a particular activity although they are not good at it. What do you do? Do you tell them not to join the soccer team because they are not well coordinated? Or should they avoid the Cub Scouts because they become overwhelmed in large groups? One way to deal with the issue is to reinforce effort. Praise your child and his efforts, not necessarily the end result. He may never meet his or your expectations, but he'll be more apt to succeed if his efforts are rewarded. Don't wait for him to reach some preconceived level of achievement—he may never reach it. But if you appreciate and praise small successes, he may achieve more than you'd expect.

Ask Your Child What Activities She Wants to Participate In

This advice seems simple, but too often we forget the obvious. A child will be more interested in participating in something she enjoys. Discuss any potential obstacles and how they can be overcome. Most important, if it doesn't work out, allow your child to withdraw.

51

Parents also need to encourage and foster friendships with the vast majority of children who are not bullies. Some victims may not have the appropriate social skills necessary to develop friendships; therefore, this needs to be taught. Some children may have special educational needs that require more specific interventions for this skill. And others may lack the social perceptual skills (that is, understand social situations) necessary to develop and maintain social relationships. These concerns need to be addressed or else your child will fail and further reinforce his feelings of incompetence.

Once the above issues are addressed, there are a number of things parents can do to help their child develop friendships.

19

HELPING YOUR CHILD MAKE FRIENDS

There are a number of things parents can do to help their child make friends. They are listed below.

Help Your Child Fit In

Notice how your child's peers dress, what styles are "in" or "out," how they bring their books to school, and what they wear outside of school. Your child doesn't always have to conform and you needn't buy every item of popular clothing or accessories. Just be sensitive so that your child does not look awkward or very different from others.

One child wanted a specific type of shorts for school and his parents didn't understand the importance of them. Finally, they gave in. The child came home from school beaming with joy that some of his classmates commented on his shorts. When children feel that they are perceived as members of the group, their social skills can be boosted. "Fitting in" is crucial at certain ages, especially during the middle school years.

Teach the Importance of Eye Contact

Children who have a limited ability to pay attention often appear bored or uninterested because they don't make eye contact with others. It is disconcerting when you are having a conversation and the individual doesn't look at you. Early on, parents can reinforce good eye contact and listening behavior. This should be done through praise, not verbal reprimands.

Enable Your Child to Observe Facial Expressions and Body Language

As a result of social and perceptual deficits or other unknown reasons, children may have trouble identifying the feelings of others represented by their facial expressions and body language. There are numerous ways to make them aware of this through observation of real life situations, as well as through TV, movies, and books. You don't have to make every opportunity a lesson, but casually note expressions and how feelings are conveyed physically.

Be a Good Role Model

Share your experiences of making friends with your child. Explain how you select friends, how you initiate a conversation, how you interpret verbal and nonverbal cues, and what is appropriate to share with friends and what is not. The more you discuss your actions and behaviors, the more likely your child will pick up on some aspects of social skill.

Making friends—it seems so simple, yet for many children it is a problem that persists for years. It must be addressed in a systematic manner, the same as any other skill. In some cases, especially for students in the middle and high school years, parents may need to seek the help of a professional outside of the school setting for counseling or specific social skill training. For victims, the more friends they can have the more likely they will be able to avoid bullying situations.

20

~~~~~~

SOCIAL SKILLS TRAINING

M any victims lack appropriate social skills. Parents can teach their child how to engage in these skills by "working on them" at home. Parents can also encourage their school district to provide specific social skills training. And in some cases, parents may seek out a professional who provides this type of training for groups of victims.

What are social skills? The ability to understand how your behavior affects others is a social skill; knowing how to make friends is a social skill; knowing when and where to say certain things is a social skill. Children who lack these skills may be unaware of the effect of their behavior on others, say the wrong thing at the wrong time, and/or have difficulty making friends.

Over the past twenty years, a number of professionals have addressed this issue and have developed social skills training programs. These programs attempt to make children aware of their own behavior and to teach them how to act in socially appropriate ways.

Most training programs have these five basic components:

1. Provide instruction
2. Present a model

3. Rehearse
4. Provide feedback
5. Practice

Provide Instruction

Be as explicit as possible when describing the social skills you want to develop. Too often children and adolescents know what they are not supposed to do, but are vague when it comes to things they should be doing. Part of the reason for this behavior is lack of training. Social skills training forces us to identify exactly what the components of appropriate social behavior are and to describe them in a clear, unambiguous manner.

If you wanted to teach "walking assertively," you would describe a few behaviors in which you could provide instructions. For example:

1. Walk with your head up.
2. Keep your shoulders back.
3. Look straight ahead.
4. And walk at a good pace.

Present a Model

A model is a demonstration of the desired behavior. At first, demonstrate what you want your child to do so that he can copy your behavior. Keep it simple. After you demonstrate the behavior, you should attempt to use different models. Some parents have been very successful with puppets, pictures, photographs, TV, videos, and books. Try to find anything that allows you to provide examples to your child of the social skill you are teaching. When selecting a model, make sure that the most important element clearly demonstrates the skill you are teaching.

In the example of "walking assertively," parents can watch TV shows with their child and point out examples of when the characters "walk assertively." Parents can also show family videos and note those who are "walking assertively." When reading with their children, parents can point out specific characters that are depicted walking in a self-assured manner.

If there are a lot of distracters, your child might focus on these, and not on the skill you are teaching. Generally speaking, the more models you provide, the higher probability that learning will take place.

Rehearse

By rehearsing social skills, children are able to act out and practice the newly developed skill in a controlled environment. For many children, the most effective type of rehearsal is verbal and motor responding. Talk through each step of the skill and allow your child to perform it. Role-playing can also be employed at this stage. However, role-playing has to be carefully orchestrated; otherwise, it will be a useless activity. It is more than you playing a role. You should clearly specify what behaviors your child is to perform and when he should perform them. Many children respond favorably to role-playing if it is carried out with this kind of specificity.

Parents can walk in a very passive way and play that role while the child plays the assertive role. Other family members can carry out specific roles. For example, the mother and one child can role-play the bully and wait for the victims to walk past them. And the child who is the victim can walk with his father in an assertive manner past the bullies.

Provide Feedback

Without information about their performance, most children won't know how they did. This feedback is critical to the success of a social skills training program. Objective, nonevaluative feedback should be given for each task performed. Tell them what they did without criticism. Feedback can be corrective ("try to walk a little taller") and/or reinforcing ("it's great the way you are looking straight ahead"). Some children benefit from video and audiotape feedback of their performance. They may perceive this as more objective than a parent giving feedback.

Practice

Once your child has performed the behavior alone, that is, without any assistance from you, she is ready to practice it under different conditions. In the beginning stages, you should provide continuous reinforcement to ensure that the skill is learned. You may find that there are "slipups." Merely go back to the step necessary to ensure success.

Parents can take their child to a mall and practice walking assertively. Try going to a local store or supermarket and practice this skill. Attempt to practice in different settings, such as places where there are a lot of people to places where there are few, if any, people.

Another social skill that is often necessary for children who are victims is to establish eye contact with the bully. The five-step process is described below.

1. *Provide Instruction.* "When you speak to someone, look in his or her eyes. And when someone is speaking to you, look in that person's eyes."
2. *Present a Model.* There are endless examples of people using good eye contact in social settings. Parents can view movies, TV shows, and family videos; go to the beach, a restaurant, the mall, or any social setting and there will be many "models" of this social skill.
3. *Rehearse.* Parents can "role-play" a child who is looking away from someone who is talking to them. Role-play at the dinner table and alternate roles of

good eye contact and poor eye contact. Don't comment negatively when your child is not using good eye contact. The purpose is to teach the appropriate skill, not to reprimand him when he doesn't demonstrate that skill.

4. *Provide Feedback.* Videotape the dinner interaction and view it together. Let your child know when he engaged in the appropriate behavior and when he did not. Together, note what characterizes "good eye contact" from "poor eye contact."

5. *Practice.* Finally, you are ready to "go public." Reinforce all your child's attempts to use this skill. Everytime he engages in proper eye contact, let him know how pleased you are with his new behavior.

The five-step procedure is extremely useful for parents. It provides a strategy for dealing with problematic behaviors in a reasonable manner. Children respond very positively because they are not being berated for their behavior but are being taught to engage in appropriate social skills. They also like it because they are receiving reinforcement at every step.

21

~~~~~~

CHILDREN WITH SPECIAL EDUCATIONAL NEEDS: LEARNING DISABILITIES

Students with special educational needs are disproportionately victimized. The imbalance of power, be it intellectual, emotional, or physical, characterizes the bully-victim relationship. It should not be surprising, therefore, that children with special educational needs are more at risk. Two groups of students appear to have the most difficulty—those with Learning Disabilities (LD) and those with Attention Deficit Hyperactivity Disorder (ADHD). Children with LD were more likely to be passive victims and children with ADHD were oftentimes provocative victims.

The major characteristics of students with learning disabilities are listed below.

Motor Problems

Some children and adolescents with learning disabilities may have trouble with tasks involving fine or gross motor skills. Fine motor tasks involve using such things as hands and fingers, whereas gross or large motor skills involve arm and leg movements or the larger muscles of the body. Students with learning disabilities may have trouble playing with blocks, puzzles, or beads; using a spoon, fork, or knife; and coloring or copying shapes and objects. Their handwriting may be poor and they may have difficulty in activities that require coordination, such as gym, playground activities, and sports. Parents often say that their learning disabled child frequently bangs into objects, knocks things over, and is awkward.

Perceptual Deficits

Perceptual deficits can be divided into two major categories: auditory and visual. *Perception* is the interpretation of information that comes to us from our environment. If this information comes to us through our ears, it is referred to as *auditory perception;* if it comes to us through our eyes, it is referred to as *visual perception.*

Most information is not strictly visual or auditory but rather a combination of the two. Students with learning disabilities have difficulty with different components of perception. For example, they may have trouble differentiating between letters that look alike (b for d, w for m) or words that are similar (was for saw), or being able to understand what someone is saying to you when there is a lot of noise in the room.

These are just a few of the problems a learning disabled child with a perceptual deficit might experience. Early in the study of learning disabilities, many problems that students encountered were attributed to their perceptual deficits. Subsequent research has not supported such contentions, yet it is clear that these deficits do exist for some students with learning disabilities.

Attention Deficits

It is estimated that approximately one-third of all students with learning disabilities have an Attention Deficit

Disorder (ADD). Many other students with learning disabilities have other problems related to attention. ADD refers to a specific group of students who have difficulty concentrating on a task. They may or may not be hyperactive.

In order to diagnose this disorder, a child or adolescent must undergo a thorough multidisciplinary evaluation, including assessment by a medical doctor (most often a neurologist). The treatment for ADD typically includes medication, counseling, and behavior management.

For a majority of students with learning disabilities, "attending" difficulties are related to the process one engages in learning. For example, they may have difficulty staying on task or deciding what is and what is not important in a lecture or reading passage, and they may not be able to sustain attention for particular tasks. This may not happen all the time—the way it does for students with ADD—but may be related to specific tasks. Many experts believe that many, if not most, students with learning disabilities have attention problems, but most (two-thirds) are not severe enough and do not occur often enough to be diagnosed as ADD.

Memory Disabilities

Some students who have learning disabilities have difficulty with memory. For some it is short-term memory (STM). STM is, as the term suggests, short: It lasts only about 30 seconds. If you don't pay attention, or *attend* to the information coming in from the environment, you'll never get it into your short-term memory. Clearly, that is exactly what happens to many students with learning disabilities. If they attend and it goes into short-term memory, it only lasts half a minute, so they need to do something with this information in order to get it into their long-term memory (LTM). For example, you are introduced to someone at a party (STM) and you do nothing to remember the name; consequently, when you see this person the following week, you have no idea of his name. However, if you did something to remember the name when you were introduced (STM), you would have been using what psychologists call *rehearsal*, and you would have a higher probability of committing it to your LTM and being able to retrieve it when you saw the person.

Memory is a complicated process that is not completely understood by researchers. However, it is clear that students with learning disabilities need assistance in using their memories. Parents of such students say things such as "he always forgets his keys," or "he never remembers to bring home his books," or they comment on how long their child studied but still did not remember things on her test. All of these are related to memory function. Whether they represent a deficit in memory or how to use one's memory is not clear.

Language Disorders

Students with learning disabilities frequently have difficulty with the reception, processing, and expression of language. These problems appear to be persistent and continue through adulthood for about half of these students. Examples of difficulty with receptive language might include children who do not understand specific sounds, words, or sentences, or those that have difficulty understanding the structure of language. Receptive language problems always result in expressive language problems. If students do not understand what comes in, they will have problems expressing themselves (input precedes output). Some students with learning disabilities have trouble coming up with the correct words, frequently talking around something or describing it. Others may have trouble with the grammar of the language (syntax); that is, they may not use the correct sequence of words or proper noun-verb agreement. And still others will have very little to comment on about the world in which they live. They tend to say very little spontaneously and even less upon demand.

Social Perceptual Disorders

Social perception can be defined as understanding the constraints of a social situation. For many students with learning disabilities, this is a major problem.

Many parents notice that their child with a learning disability has a hard time making friends, says the wrong thing at the wrong time, does not think before he speaks, and says things most children don't say. These are just some of the characteristics of a child who has difficulty with social perceptual skills.

We probably know less about this area than other areas of deficit, but it may well be the most devastating because of its ramifications for the child or adolescent and his family.

Emotional Overlay

It is not surprising that emotional issues are closely related to having a learning disability. Children come to school wanting to succeed like everyone else. Children with learning disabilities often realize early in their school career that their best efforts don't always lead to success. Couple that with teachers and parents who may not recognize the disability, and it is obvious that undetected learning disabilities can lead to social-emotional difficulties.

Also, over the years people studying learning disabilities have concentrated on the academic aspects of the disorders. As a result, many students have carried the negative emotional baggage through adulthood.

These students do not have behavior disorders or significant emotional problems. (At least they didn't when they began their school career.) However, many professionals recognize that it does not take long before it is impossible to detect which disorder came first.

Clearly these characteristics can make these children extremely vulnerable and therefore easily victimized. Because they are high risk they should be identified by school staff and provided with strategies for dealing with bullies. They may need additional instructions and specific methods of instruction. Consult with the director of special education and the special education staff in order to develop an appropriate plan.

22

CHILDREN WITH SPECIAL EDUCATIONAL NEEDS: ATTENTION DEFICIT DISORDERS

Commonly cited characteristics of children with ADD are *hyperactivity*, *distractibility*, and *impulsivity*. Children with ADD have difficulty staying on task and focusing on important aspects of conversations or school-related tasks. Frequently, they do not complete tasks because they are moving rapidly from one activity to another or are distracted by extraneous stimuli.

Hyperactivity is a specific central nervous system disorder that makes it difficult for children to control their motor activity. These children may not be constantly on the go, but they appear restless and fidgety. Parents may say that their child can't sit through a meal, moves from one activity to another very rapidly, or "never shuts up." Teachers describe these students as always doing something. They often get up to sharpen their pencil, tap their pencil or their fingers on the desk, or tap their foot on the floor. They finish assignments quickly and often incorrectly, run around on the playground, or squirm at their desks.

These behaviors often have no purpose or focus. An observer may say "I don't know where he gets his energy" or "I wish I had his energy." Yet this is not the type of energy that allows someone to accomplish a great deal. Quite the opposite, it interferes with productivity. The term *hyperactive* is overused. Many children and adolescents should not be referred to as hyperactive. The term should not be used casually, but reserved for those children and adolescents with a specific disorder. Without a multidisciplinary evaluation, including a medical evaluation, it is difficult to judge a child's movements as hyperactive.

Some children may not be hyperactive but may have great difficulty staying on task. These children are easily distracted and struggle to filter information that comes in via the senses. Most people can block out certain bits of information from the environment and focus on what is important. Unfortunately, children who are distractible are not good at discriminating between relevant and irrelevant information, thus everything competes for their attention. They are unable to focus on a specific task for a long period of time, thus *short attention span* is often used to describe them.

Children and adolescents who are easily distracted can be bothered by a slight noise in another part of the room. They may hear someone talking outside the house and be distracted by it. A car goes by the window and they rush to look out. They may walk into the bedroom to get something, their attention shifts to a picture on the wall, and they forget why they went into the bedroom. Many of these children experience difficulty in places where a great deal is going on, such as a birthday parties, shopping malls, and carnivals. They can become irritable and restless because of the increased stimulation in their surroundings. Some classrooms can cause the same problem when so much is going on that the child can't attend effectively.

Some children with ADD are impulsive. They act first and think later. They may say things that are offensive, but not realize it until it is pointed out to them. A youngster may even hit his classmates frequently and then apologize profusely. Afterward, he is unable to understand the meaning of his behavior and he merely acts out. Impulsive children ask questions that have nothing to do with the conversation at hand. In class, these children call out answers before the questions have been asked (and they are usually the wrong answers).

Such impulsive children and adolescents appear to be accident-prone because they do not attend to the consequences of their actions. Some children have jumped out of windows, fallen out of trees, and run through glass doors. Many get an incredible number of cuts, scratches, and bruises.

The behavior of the child who truly has ADD will be manifested in both school and home. If a child only displays these characteristics in one such setting, then it can probably be attributed to causes other than ADD. Clearly, these students will engage in behavior that will be provocative. Parents and teachers must be aware of the nature of this disorder so that these children will not be victimized.

Part Five

WHAT YOU CAN DO IF YOUR CHILD IS A BULLY

P arents of bullies are provided with specific techniques that they can use with their children. Additionally, they are provided with guidelines they can use to determine if they need to seek professional help.

23

EARLY IDENTIFICATION AND INTERVENTION

P arents need to be able to identify characteristics in order to provide effective interventions at an early age.

Some of the possible signs that a child may be a bully include:
- Constant teasing of other children
- Intimidating others, making fun of, ridiculing others
- Acts of physical aggression toward others
- Being "bossy"
- Picking on children smaller and weaker than themselves
- Getting other children to do these things to smaller and weaker children; manipulation of others
- Being physically stronger than their classmates and their victims in particular; may be the same age as or somewhat older than their victims; are physically effective in play activities, sports, and fights (applies particularly to boys)
- Having strong needs to dominate and subdue other students, to assert themselves with power and threat, and to get their own way; they may brag about their actual or imagined superiority over other students
- Being hot-tempered, easily angered, impulsive, and having low frustration tolerance; they have difficulty conforming

to rules and tolerating adversities and delays, and may try to gain advantage by cheating

- Being generally oppositional, defiant, and aggressive toward adults (including teachers and parents) and possibly frightening also to adults (depending upon the age and physical strength of the young person); being good at talking themselves out of "difficult situations"
- Being seen as tough and hardened, and showing little empathy with students who are victimized
- Not being anxious or insecure and typically having a relatively positive view of themselves (average or better than average self-esteem)
- Engaging at a relatively early age (as compared with their peers) in other antisocial behaviors including stealing, vandalism, and getting drunk; associating with "bad companions"
- Being average, above, or below average in popularity among their classmates, but often having support from at least a small number of peers; in middle school, bullying students are likely to be less popular than in primary school
- With regard to school achievement, being average, above, or below average in elementary school, whereas in middle school they usually (but not necessarily) get lower grades and develop a negative attitude to school

It is not bullying if a child engages in one of these behaviors infrequently. The nature of bullying is a persistent pattern. Children who are bullies engage in this behavior over and over and over again. Parents of bullies frequently report that they have spoken to their children, punished them, and taken away favorite toys, and they still continued picking on others.

Parents report that their children do not appear to be remorseful when they are confronted. This has also been evident in the research on bullying. Bullies like the payoffs of physical aggression and intimidation and, despite what many people think, they have friends and have good self-esteem, at least in the early grades. This tends to fade as bullies go through the middle grades and high school. It is so important for parents to be aware of the possible signs of bullying and to find the appropriate help.

Many parents may, unwittingly, reinforce bullying by their own behavior. Parents need to employ nonaggressive child-rearing techniques. Just because your child was involved in a bullying incident does not mean that he or she is a bully. However, if there are repeated incidents reported in school and/or by other parents, you need to examine the situation carefully.

At first glance, it appears that the victims are the worst off, especially when you read the terrible accounts of victimization. Obviously, victimization is so severe at times to push someone to suicide. But, bullies also suffer a great deal in the long run. They tend to be underdeveloped academically and socially and unemployed, and have a high probability of being involved in criminal behavior. Therefore, it is wise to treat bullying incidents with the seriousness they deserve. When parents and schools work together, there have been positive results.

24

BE AN APPROPRIATE ROLE MODEL

C learly there are influences from society that have an impact on our children. And there are temperamental differences among all children that make some children more apt to engage in certain types of behavior. Yet, in the case of bullying, the style of "parenting" is also an area of concern. Parents need to be appropriate role models for conflict resolution, for treating others with respect and care and for reinforcing their child's appropriate behaviors and establishing clear-cut consequences for inappropriate behaviors. This Key will focus on the first aspect—role models. Parenting is a lot of work. No doubt the rewards far outweigh the work for most of us, but it's still work. Many parents have said that they never realized how careful they have to be in what they say and what they do because their kids will "throw it back" to them. Below are a few scenarios that discuss options available to parents and how each opinion might affect their child or children.

Scenario 1

You and your family are waiting on a line in a department store and someone bumps into you. Immediately you tell that person to be careful and watch where she is walking. She apologizes, but you continue to speak in a harsh voice because you want to make your point that the person should be more careful. At this point, there are quite a few people staring at you, and the person walks away. You turn to your family and with a satisfied look on your face you say, "You have to let people know what you think."

Parents may think that this forceful approach to the outside world shows children that it is important to stick up for yourself. What it will likely teach children who are prone to bullying is that you need to constantly berate someone so that they will submit to you. It also shows children that every act should be perceived as a provocation. And, finally, creating the chaotic situation in a store full of people is something to be valued—who cares if "people are looking; that's their problem" is an attitude that might be instilled.

An alternative to the above is to merely accept the apology and move on. It shows your children that people aren't perfect, sometimes people are inattentive, but it's not a big deal—be apologetic and it's over. Even if she didn't apologize, you can simply ignore the behavior and perhaps tell your kids to be careful—sometimes people don't pay attention as they run through stores.

Scenario 2

You are out for a drive with your family and someone cuts you off. You scream at them, rush to pull up alongside of their car, start screaming at them and give them an obscene hand gesture, and drive off mumbling what a bunch of jerks are on the roads these days.

Some people feel a sense of empowerment when they are in a car. In a well-publicized case in the New York City area, a couple, with an infant in the car, was cut off by another car and gave the driver an obscene gesture. The car caught up to them and its driver shot and killed the other driver's wife and baby. This is clearly an extreme, but if you needed a reason to be passive in a car, then this is it.

Relatively calm people become very aggressive when driving, if they perceive a violation of the rules of the road. A mother of a three year old reported that her daughter corrected her when a car stopped abruptly in front of her. The mother yelled, "you stupid jerk" and the daughter said, "No, Mommy" you're supposed to say "you (expletive deleted) jerk." This child learned that was the typical response her mother made when this happened.

It's not wrong to get annoyed. What is clearly inappropriate is to try to resolve this issue through aggression on the road. Why not assume that the driver did not do this intentionally, beep your horn, and move on (literally). Not too long ago, we were hit by an 18-wheel Mack truck. It sideswiped our car on an interstate highway. Fortunately, we were fine and the car was driveable, but it was clearly upsetting. Well, as we pulled along the side of the highway, the driver of the truck emerged from his cab and the first thing he said was "I'm sorry buddy, I just didn't see you." What could I say? We sat in the car, waited for the police, and realized that's why it is called an accident.

Scenario 3

Your child describes a scene at school where he characterizes one classmate as a "real dork" whom everyone makes fun of. He tells you how he looks so "out of it" in his peculiar clothes and "weird" habits. You merely continue eating as he describes the rest of his day in school.

By ignoring these remarks, you are letting your child know that it's okay to make fun of someone, to ridicule the person, and to call him names. Kids will do this occasionally, but it is still important for parents to make a clear statement that it is not acceptable. Depending on your child's age, you might say, "It's really not nice to make fun of someone" or "It must be hard for this kid" or "I'm sure there is something you could like about him" or "Why don't you be nice to him and maybe others will do the same" and the like. You need to let your children know at an early age that this is unacceptable behavior.

Scenario 4

You are in a restaurant when you overhear the conversation at the table next to you. The people are verbally abusive to the waitress and you really don't know what the problem is, but it appears to be escalating, and the waitress appears to be overwhelmed.

If you choose to do nothing and act as if it never happened, you might be teaching your child to not get involved. Too much bullying occurs because the "silent majority" of children allow it to go on. Verbal intervention may not be appropriate because the bullies at the table will probably tell you to mind your own business. However, you can very matter-of-factly find the manager of the restaurant and let him or her know that the waitress needs assistance immediately. This serves as a model for your child to tell a teacher when he or she feels someone is being picked on and not to merely ignore it.

Scenario 5

Your children are arguing over the use of a toy. You tell them that if they keep it up neither one of them will be able to play with it. They continue arguing and you angrily grab the toy, break it, throw it in the garbage, slap both children and send them to their rooms.

This is an obvious one. You lose your temper and become physically aggressive toward your children. When they lose their temper, they will become aggressive toward each other and other children. Physical punishment should never be used. The only thing it teaches children is that it's okay to hit people. An alternative would be to simply remove the toy and have them "earn it" back in a few days. If the fighting continues, remove them from the room. But it is more important to use reinforcement when children are good. This will be discussed in the next Key.

It's not easy being a role model, but you are one. You must recognize that every time you interact with your children, you are teaching them something. As they observe the way you resolve conflicts both in and out of the home and family, they will begin to use these strategies with others. If these strategies are perceived as bullying, they will bully others to get their way. Just as bullies can learn these behaviors from their parents, parents of bullies can learn to replace these behaviors with more effective conflict resolution and parenting techniques.

25

USE OF REINFORCEMENT

Reinforcement is defined as anything that increases the strength of a behavior. If your child does something that pleases you and you praise her for it, she does it again. The more powerful the reinforcer, the more likely the behavior will occur again. People respond to different types of reinforcers, for example, some of us respond to pay, others to food, and still others to a simple "thank-you." Nevertheless, there are some general guidelines that should be used when delivering reinforcement. The first thing you need to do is to start simply. The hierarchy of reinforcement is listed below.

1. Praise (verbal and nonverbal)
2. Praise coupled with activities
3. Praise coupled with tangible rewards
4. Token economy systems

Step one is to use praise. Too often, parents think that reinforcement requires them to give their child expensive toys or gifts every time they do something appropriate. Although some type of tangible reward may be necessary for some children, one of the most effective ways to increase appropriate attending behavior is to praise (verbally and nonverbally) your child after she engages in appropriate behavior.

Early research findings in this area provided parents with a simple dictum: "Catch them when they're good." It was clear that the more parents commented on their child's positive behavior, the more the child displayed the behavior. It sounds so simple, but it's not. Parents may be so attuned to focusing on negative behavior that they find the shift in focus very difficult. Some parents may find it awkward praising their children for appropriate behaviors. Some parents feel especially uncomfortable when praising their child outside of the home. Why, they wonder, do they have to praise desired behavior when other parents don't? And moreover, others look at them in disbelief. The professional literature and our experiences indicate that initially it is awkward and at times, uncomfortable to be so effusive in your praise. Yet, when you start receiving results, it becomes worth it. A step-by-step guide to delivering praise is as follows:

1. Make a list of all appropriate behaviors your child engages in, no matter how simple they appear to be. Take nothing for granted. The easiest way to do this is to write down during a typical day every appropriate behavior from the time your child awakens until she goes to sleep. If both parents are available, both should make lists. Do this independent of each other. You'd be surprised how much each of you miss.

2. Every time your child displays the targeted behavior, say and/or do something positive. Try to vary your comments so that you are not continually saying "good." It's helpful if you can be specific in your praise. For example, "I like the way you treated Michael, you really made me proud." Smiles, winks, and hugs should also be used frequently.

3. Praise should be delivered only after your child displays the appropriate behavior. You are trying to establish a link between the behavior and the

consequence. If you praise her when she is engaging in inappropriate behaviors, you will increase them, which is exactly the opposite of what you are attempting to do.

4. Praise should be delivered very often in the beginning of a behavioral program. This continuous reinforcement serves to strengthen a behavior. As the behavior occurs more often, you can gradually reduce praise.

5. Praise should be delivered immediately after the behavior occurs in the beginning stages. Every time a positive behavior occurs, praise should be given. Over time, you will be able to reduce the frequency of praise, but not until the behavior has been clearly established.

6. Praise should be genuine. Most parents we know are truly pleased when their child engages in appropriate behavior. Their praise merely reflects this. If you use praise in an artificial manner, children will see through it.

7. If you find it difficult to give praise, try some of these tips:

   a. Post signs around the house (especially in the cupboards in the kitchen) to serve as reminders. (Example: Don't forget to let Adam know how much you appreciate his "caring behavior.")

   b. Tape-record segments of the day and play it back in order to monitor your rate of praise.

   c. Buy a wrist golf counter and record your behavior each day. Try to increase it by 10 percent daily.

   d. Put a piece of adhesive tape on your wrist and make a mark each time you praise your child.

Praise will not be effective for every behavior associated with aggressive behavior. You may need to use additional reinforcers. What it will do, however, is reduce many minor disruptive behaviors and highlight those behaviors that may need additional reinforcement. Without this clarity, every behavior takes on the same value. After awhile, physically abusing one's siblings becomes as important as not being ready when the school bus arrives. Even when praise alone is ineffective, it should not be abandoned. You merely couple praise with the additional reinforcers noted above.

The next step in the hierarchy is praise coupled with activities. These activities should be ones readily available in your home; you should not have to go out and buy lavish rewards. Merely write down all the activities your child finds pleasurable. Every time they engage in the appropriate behavior, have them "earn" the activity. These should be somewhat simple, such as being read to, watching TV, playing ball, playing a board game. Essentially, children learn that first they do something that you want them to do, then they receive something they want.

Parents find this procedure to be very effective. You are not using threats ("Remember, if you want to play ball . . ."). Rather, you are allowing them to "earn" privileges when they engage in appropriate behaviors. Once again, this may not be effective for all behaviors. If this does not work, proceed to the next step in the hierarchy.

Praise coupled with tangible reinforcement. This type of reinforcement may be necessary for some children. As noted above, praise should be continued and coupled with a tangible reinforcement immediately after the behavior occurs. Try to think of all the tangible rewards your child likes. These can be stickers, pencils, pads, food, or any small item your child enjoys. Use only small amounts. Try to spread the rewards throughout the day. In many cases, parents benefit from consultation with a professional well versed in applied behavior analysis techniques at this point. The use of tangible rewards needs to be closely monitored.

A *token economy system* may also be appropriate, that is, implementing a system whereby your child earns points, stars, tokens, and similar items that can be traded in a later date for specified reinforcements. Some children and adolescents benefit from the use of contracts, that is, when a parent and child develop an agreement specifying what each must do. Although these contracts are not impossible to carry out on your own, it is wise to consult a professional. Once you are able to develop the skills necessary to carry out such programs, the quicker you will see changes in your child's behavior. And you are more apt to develop such skills under the guidance of a professional.

Some parents may have a hard time coming up with potential reinforcers for their children. For suggestions, refer to Appendix A: Types of Reinforcers.

26

EFFECTIVE USE OF PUNISHMENT

Reinforcement does not always work. There are times when a negative consequence needs to be applied in order to change a behavior. And in many cases, the combination of high rates of reinforcements and low rates of punishment may be the most effective solution of all.

Anything that decreases a behavior is defined as a *punisher*. This does not include any form of physical punishment, usually known as corporal punishment. Spanking or hitting any child or adolescent is wrong for a number of reasons. To intentionally inflict physical harm on another human being is inexcusable. The message to children is clear: Those bigger and stronger and more powerful than you can get you to do what they want by force. It is not surprising that children and adolescents then choose this as a strategy for dealing with others. From a behavioral point of view, spanking and hitting are ineffective and teach our children and adolescents the wrong behavior. Children and adolescents learn from our behavior; parents must demonstrate civilized ways of dealing with conflict.

It is difficult dealing with inappropriate behaviors that occur frequently day in and day out. However, there are effective alternative methods available to parents. If you feel that you are in danger of employing corporal punishment with your child, you may need to seek help to resolve this problem.

As with reinforcement, there is a hierarchy in the use of punishment. Too often, parents escalate their response rapidly and go from telling a child to "stop that!" to sending him to his room for an interminable period of time. There are several intermediate steps:

1. Ignore inappropriate behaviors
2. Verbal reprimands
3. Removal of privileges
4. Time-out

Parents are often told to "ignore it and it will go away." It's not so simple. *Ignoring inappropriate behaviors* is a very effective technique but one that many parents find difficult to implement. The technical phrase used to describe ignoring is "time-out from social reinforcement." The idea is that there is reinforcement occurring in the child's environment and the absence of this reinforcement (ignoring) will encourage the child to engage in the appropriate behavior to receive reinforcement. This process is also hard to carry out. Parents are often frustrated by their inability to ignore inappropriate behaviors. Here are a few suggestions:

1. Never stand there staring at your child while he engages in the behavior.
2. Go to another room.
3. Listen to music. A Walkman is helpful.
4. Keep busy—cook, read, and so forth.
5. Use "self-talk." Tell yourself that the behavior will pass and this is an effective procedure.
6. Husbands and wives should assist each other as they ignore inappropriate behaviors.

Don't be surprised if the behavior increases at first. Think about it. How many times have you not paid attention to (ignored) a behavior, but it finally got to you and you responded. Your child asks you for a cookie before dinner, you say, "No." He continues to ask, the request now becoming incessant. Finally, you scream, "Take the cookie and let me finish making dinner!" It's easy to do, we've done it more than a few times. Unfortunately, that only teaches children that the longer they persist and the more annoying they can become, the more likely you will give in to their request. So it's not surprising that in the initial stages of ignoring, your child will continue to pursue the previously learned strategy. Just try to sustain the ignoring until you see a change in behavior. Do not ignore behaviors that are injurious to your child or anybody else, or destructive to property, however.

Ignoring is most effective when used in combination with reinforcement of the desired behavior. Your child should get your attention when engaging in desirable, not undesirable, behavior.

Ignoring is hard and may take a long time to decrease a behavior. Also, it is probably the most effective for behaviors that are reinforced by verbal and nonverbal praise. Because it is hard to ignore behaviors, this technique is often not employed to its maximum usefulness. On the other hand, there are many behaviors that will not be changed merely by systematically ignoring them and you may have to proceed to Step 2 (verbal reprimands).

Verbal reprimands should be kept small and to the point. Too much discussion of the inappropriate behavior may only serve to increase or maintain it. For example, the reasons why the child should not engage in the behavior, its effect on you, on the child, or on other members of the household, and so forth, will not be understood. Rather than saying, "I must have told you one thousand times not to interrupt me when I'm using the food processor. Don't you realize I could get hurt? Can't you just wait like everyone else? I'll never get this done if you keep interrupting me," a simple "no," "enough," "stop," "please don't do that" will suffice. Once the child engages in the appropriate behavior, reinforce her.

Many times verbal reprimands go unheeded and you need to move to Step 3, *removal of privileges*. This is not done in haste ("That's it, you're not leaving the house today" or "Forget about going to the beach tomorrow"). It should be carried out in a well-thought-out manner, and the ground rules should be discussed with your child. She should know that if she engages in a specified behavior, she will not get certain rewards. The underlying principle is that children are always earning reinforcements; when they display certain undesirable behaviors, these reinforcements are unattainable. This procedure can be used with verbal reprimands if necessary.

If all of the above steps fail to decrease inappropriate behaviors, you may need to employ other more complex procedures, such as *time-out*. These are best undertaken with the advice of a professional trained in applied behavior analysis. The program must be developed, implemented, and monitored in a systematic fashion.

There are a few cautions about the use of punishment. According to the professional literature, most interaction between parent and child is negative. That is, parents tend to comment much more on the negative than the positive behaviors that their children engage in. Therefore, punishment must be used sparingly and with high rates of verbal and nonverbal praise and other reinforcements. If delivered out of frustration and anger and employed excessively, punishment will not change behaviors.

27

KNOW WHEN TO SEEK PROFESSIONAL HELP

It is very difficult to change your own behavior. Parents have come to think that they should know exactly what to do and when to do it and to do otherwise is to admit failure. Parents can learn effective parenting techniques in order to reduce the bullying behaviors of their children. They can change the behavior of their children.

There are times, however, when it's difficult to do it alone. You may need to seek the assistance of a professional. Knowing when to do so is critical. Below are a number of situations that will probably need the assistance of a professional.

- *If you feel you can't control yourself and you want to hit your child.* This is the number one reason why you should seek the help of a professional. Recently, a parent described an incident where she was riding on the bus with her eight-year-old daughter who would not stop crying and the mother said, "I thought that if I just hit her head against the pole on the bus she'd stop. I came very close to doing it." These feelings—that the only way to stop a behavior is to use physical (corporal) punishment—must be dealt with immediately. You don't have to go far to read of cases where parents have killed their children because they felt they had no alternative. If you consider using force to stop a behavior or if you frequently hit your child now—get help and get it soon. Call the child protective services agency in your area or call the school and ask for the name of a professional who works with parents and contact them immediately.

- *If you see your child being physically abusive toward others.* If your child is frequently observed "hitting" others and does not appear to be remorseful, seek help. Bullying occurs more frequently in school settings, so many parents say they've never observed their child bullying anybody. Therefore, if you see your child hitting others, biting others, and, in general, inflicting harm when you have children over, at birthday parties, or at the playground, seek professional help—this is a serious problem.

- *If your child is involved with the police.* If your child has been involved in criminal behavior, such as robbing, beating up, or threatening others, and has been arrested, this is clearly something serious and help should be obtained as soon as possible. The bullying cycle starts early, but without intervention, there is an increased risk of criminal behavior.

- *If you are frequently contacted by the school.* If you receive a number of complaints from school officials that your child has been bullying other children, it is usually a real concern. A few instances are not a problem. But when a child is targeted by the school as a bully, parental intervention is critical. This is especially true if the school doesn't have a good anti-bully program, which is the next reason to seek professional help.

- *If your school doesn't have a comprehensive plan to deal with bullying.* If you recognize the fact that your child is a bully, yet the school has no consistent way of dealing with bullies and their victims, you must seek the help of a professional outside of the school. Although more schools are addressing this issue, it continues to be an area of relative neglect in the United States. You should advocate to have a school-wide program developed and implemented, but in the interim, get help for your child.

- *You've tried some techniques but they just didn't work.* You have conscientiously tried to change your parenting techniques, but you have been unsuccessful. This happens to many parents. You need to relearn how to be an effective parent, and that takes time and effort. You may enroll in a "parenting" course but feel you need more specific, individualized assistance. You may try to carry out some of the procedures, like a contract or a token economy system, but it's just not working. There are many parents who truly try to change their own behavior but cannot do it without the assistance of a professional. And this is not long-term psychotherapy; this is goal-directed counseling and/or specific behavioral intervention that helps parents of bullies change their parenting style. This, coupled with a school-based program, is very effective.

Part Six

WHAT SCHOOLS CAN DO ABOUT BULLYING

I magine the confusion that a child would experience if his parents and his teacher told him two entirely different ways of dealing with a particular situation. The child tells the teacher he is being bullied and the teacher provides him with a number of strategies to deal with the problem that don't include using physical force. The child is also enrolled in a school that has developed a school-wide program to deal with bullying and there are clearly established rules and consequences.

When he goes home, he tells his parents about the bully and they tell him to "stand up to him or he'll walk all over you. Fight back!" What is the child supposed to do? This is just one example of the confusing and conflicting messages students will receive if parents and schools don't work together.

Parents should be involved from the early stages of any program that deals with bullying. Schools can send a letter home requesting parents' input, provide the Parent-Teacher Organizations with requests for input, and reach out to parents who have asked the school for help with bullying. Parents need to be provided with basic information about the nature of bullying, including suggestions for dealing with the problem at home. They need to know the school rules and consequences for bullying, and they need to be informed if any changes occur.

This section will provide parents with the major components of a school-wide program so that they can serve as advocates for their children and encourage school personnel to carry out such a program.

28

SCHOOLS—
FERTILE GROUNDS
FOR BULLYING

Schools must do something about bullying. Most bullying occurs to students in transit to and from school and in the unstructured, unsupervised areas in and around schools. Children report that they are called names when they wait for the school bus, some are jostled and have lunch taken away from them on the way to school, and others report that their lockers are broken into, lunch money stolen, and belongings destroyed. Students report that they eat alone because no one will sit with them. And when they go to recess, they stay in an isolated section of the school yard. These isolated sections of the playground, school yards, and hallways in schools become fertile ground for physical abuse of victims by bullies.

Many victims have a variety of physical and psychological ailments, such as fainting, vomiting, paralysis, hyperventilation, visual problems, headaches, stomachaches, and hysteria. They have frequent absences from school as a result of these ailments or out of sheer fear. These are directly related to the presence of bullies in their schools.

The view that this is typical child's play is changing somewhat, but not fast enough. There are some excellent programs for schools (See Appendix D: Resources for Schools), but they are not employed in enough schools. One of the most startling findings from the research on bullying is that victims of bullies feel that schools didn't do anything about it. Most students feel they have no one to go to if they are victimized.

One middle school youngster reported that a bully cut in front of him every day on the lunch line. When he told his teacher, the teacher told him to work it out. This same child was a victim of physical aggression in the classroom. Whenever his math teacher would write an example on the board, a bully would slap this child on the head. When the teacher turned around, the bully stopped. The victim told the teacher what had happened and the teacher replied, "What can I do if I don't see it?" Not surprisingly, when the child's parent told him to tell the adult in charge that he's being picked on, he simply said, "Why, they don't do anything."

29

EARLY IDENTIFICATION OF BULLIES AND THEIR VICTIMS

B efore any program can be developed, there should be a needs assessment, which is critical in order to understand the nature of bullying in your school. Parents and schools can collaboratively develop one for your school or you can use one that is already available. One such questionnaire, referred to as *My Life in School*, was developed by Sonia Sharp, Tiny Arora, Peter K. Smith, and Irene Whitney of the Division of Education, University of Sheffield (England).

Once the students complete this questionnaire, evaluate the results. An informal tally of the specific incidents will provide information on the frequency and types of bullying incidents in the building. Further analysis may be necessary to look at specific grades and classrooms. This should be undertaken in a collaborative manner, with parents and schools working together.

MY LIFE IN SCHOOL

I am a Boy   I am a Girl   Age   Year

DURING THIS WEEK IN SCHOOL, ANOTHER CHILD:	NOT AT ALL	ONCE	MORE THAN ONCE
1. Called me names			
2. Said something nice to me			
3. Was nasty about my family			
4. Tried to kick me			
5. Was very nice to me			
6. Was unkind because I am different			
7. Gave me a present			
8. Said they'd beat me up			
9. Gave me some money			
10. Tried to make me give them money			
11. Tried to frighten me			
12. Asked me a stupid question			
13. Lent me something			
14. Stopped me playing a game			
15. Was unkind about something I did			
16. Talked about clothes with me			

DURING THIS WEEK IN SCHOOL, ANOTHER CHILD:	NOT AT ALL	ONCE	MORE THAN ONCE
17. Told me a joke			
18. Told me a lie			
19. Got a gang on me			
20. Tried to make me hurt other people			
21. Smiled at me			
22. Tried to get me into trouble			
23. Helped me carry something			
24. Tried to hurt me			
25. Helped me with my class work			
26. Made me do something I didn't want to do			
27. Talked about TV with me			
28. Took something off me			
29. Shared something with me			
30. Was rude about the color of my skin			
31. Shouted at me			
32. Played a game with me			
33. Tried to trip me up			
34. Talked about things I like			

DURING THIS WEEK IN SCHOOL, ANOTHER CHILD:	NOT AT ALL	ONCE	MORE THAN ONCE
35. Laughed at me horribly			
36. Said they would tell on me			
37. Tried to break something of mine			
38. Told a lie about me			
39. Tried to hit me			

97

30

DEVELOPING AND IMPLEMENTING SCHOOL-WIDE PROGRAMS

A recent article in the *New York Times* describes how a superintendent of schools planned to address the "bully problem." He assured members of the community that he would not tolerate such behavior and that the bullies would be identified and suspended. Sounds like an aggressive, no-nonsense approach to a significant issue. The only problem is that it won't work. Bullying is much too complex an issue to be dealt with by administrative fiat. The most effective programs appear to be ones in which there is a school-wide program that is developed in a collaborative manner by the school and the community.

The goals of a school-wide program are twofold: (1) to reduce, if not eliminate the bully/victim problem in and out of school, and (2) to prevent future incidents of bullying. Victims need to feel safe in school and bullies need to learn how to assert themselves in more socially acceptable ways.

All school personnel and community members need to become aware of the serious nature of bullying. One way to do this is to administer to students a questionnaire on bullying. Once schools have developed an awareness of the problem, they will be able to address it. Without such an awareness, they will resort to ineffective, outdated interventions that have little, if any, chance of success.

Most school-wide programs have three major components: (1) clear-cut rules, (2) reinforcement for those students who obey these rules, and (3) consequences for not following the rules. These must be adhered to by the entire school staff, as well as by community members.

The first step in implementing a program is to provide training for the school staff. As previously noted, many parents and teachers do not recognize the severity of the bullying problem. Children who are bullied frequently report that they cannot depend on adults in authority positions to do anything about the problem. Therefore, the first step is awareness. Typically, bullying is much more pervasive than most teachers thought. Once they recognize the nature of the problem, they are ready to learn how to deal with it.

Training should provide appropriate role models, intervention strategies, and support for victims. Additionally, staff members can use literature or videos as a supplement. There are a number of books that provide excellent examples of dealing with bullies and empathizing with the victims, and preventive strategies, as well as videos that do the same. (A listing of these can be found in Appendix C: Resources for Schools.)

What can teachers do to reduce bullying in their classrooms? As previously noted, a school-wide approach is necessary to change the school environment, but the individual teacher is critical for the success of any program. Just as parents model appropriate behavior in their home, teachers do so in their classes. Classrooms where teachers provide a warm, supportive environment and clear and consistent rules regarding bullying send a strong message to their students. Teachers must be aware of the characteristics of bullies and their victims and know when and where to get help in their school and their community.

Verbal reinforcement (praise) of kind acts toward others is one way to demonstrate to students that it is okay to treat others with respect and dignity. Praise those students who engage in this behavior.

There are a few guidelines for the effective use of praise in the classroom. They include:

- Teachers' praise should be delivered only after the student displays the appropriate behavior. The teacher should try to establish a link between the behavior and the consequence. If a student is praised when she is engaging in inappropriate behaviors, these behaviors will increase.
- Praise should be delivered very often in the beginning of a behavioral program. This continuous reinforcement serves to strengthen a behavior. As the behavior occurs more often, gradually reduce praise.
- Praise should be delivered immediately after the behavior occurs in the beginning stages. Every time a positive behavior occurs, praise should be given. Over time, reduce the frequency of praise, but not until the behavior has been clearly established.
- Praise should be genuine. Most teachers are truly pleased when their students engage in appropriate behavior. Their praise merely reflects this.

Facial expressions and body language also provide powerful nonverbal models of behavior for students. Teachers may inadvertently give the message, through looks like rolling of the eyes, that this student is a pain in the neck and deserves the negative treatment from his or her classmates. This is particularly true for provocative victims. There was one incident where a young girl was frequently the recipient of verbal taunts from her peers. They commented on everything from how slow she was to how she never listened and on and on. When the classroom teacher was observed, it was clear that the teacher found the girl's behavior annoying and, in many ways, gave the class license to bully this student. There is good news and bad news about this incident. The good news is that the teacher was able to change her own behavior and eliminate these negative nonverbal statements about this student. The bad news is that the pattern of behavior was established and that it followed this child from class to lunch to playground.

If a child is a loner, which many victims are, a classroom teacher can find something the child does well and have him or her work with other students who are not as competent. A teacher could place this child in a group with some cooperative, empathetic students who would work together and include him or her in the group. Groups can receive reinforcement for cooperative behaviors and point out how the child who is the victim performed so well. The teacher can try to make this child attractive to be with either by his or her competence or by reinforcement of his or her group. Over time, there is a higher probability that kids will involve this child in their group.

Victims of bullying are not terribly competent in athletic endeavors, so they are usually the last selected. Many readers of this book will readily identify with those children who are always left out. There is absolutely no reason why this has to happen in a school setting. This is a controlled environment. Teachers should not allow students to select their partners, their groups, their teams, because, invariably, children who are passive victims will not get selected. There are children who have never been selected as lab partners and when the teacher finds them a partner, the partner moans in disgust. This happens day in, day out. Random selections of partners or teachers placing a victim with a popular child can eliminate this humiliating experience. And clear and consistent consequences for negative behaviors of other students must be provided.

There are children who eat lunch every day by themselves. They then go out to the playground for recess, by themselves. Someone has to notice this, but what is done about it? Teachers can provide some supervision in the lunchroom, assign seats, and/or reinforce those children who eat in a cooperative manner. They can also find some caring youngster who would include the isolated child in their group. Attention must be paid to those situations that allow for the inappropriate isolation of victimized students.

Teachers need to send unambiguous messages to all of their students that all children in their class are valued and that respect for each other is expected, and reinforced.

Recently there have been reports in the professional literature regarding teachers who are bullies. Although only a small percent have been noted, there needs to be further exploration of this problem. Finally, there are teachers who clearly scapegoat children or have favorites. This will influence the dynamics of the classroom and allow the bullying process to continue. Teacher behavior will frequently dictate student behavior.

31

INSURING SUPPORT FOR VICTIMS

Schools must insure support for victims. Victims must know whom to go to for help and that help will be available. They also need to know that it is not a sign of weakness to ask for help. Yet an untapped source of support for victims is the overwhelming majority of students not directly involved in the bully/victim scenario. This so-called "silent majority" needs to be encouraged and supported for providing support to victims. By not doing so, they are unwittingly providing support for the bully. Dr. John H. Hoover, an Associate Professor of Special Education at the University of North Dakota, Grand Forks, has described his reason for studying bullying. In a candid article in *Reclaiming Children and Youth,** he describes his experience.

Miss Torgerson would leave the room unattended for 15 minutes each day for coffee and, I suspect, a quick cigarette. She and the other teachers most likely needed to unwind from mornings locked into chambers with 40 preteens. The weekly class president was put in charge, ostensibly to write scoundrels' names on the board for later adjudication. The result frequently was chaotic.

---

*From "Why I Study Bullying" by John H. Hoover, in *Reclaiming Children and Youth: Journal of Emotional and Behavioral Problems* 5 (1): 10–11 (spring, 1996). Reprinted by permission of JEB-P, Inc.

Absent Miss Torgerson's calming presence, students vaulted over desks, yelled exuberantly, and knocked books out of one another's hands. A few might play a board game in one corner, while a small minority attempted to work quietly. We posted a lookout at the door to warn about the advent of teachers or the principal.

Diane joined our class in mid-September. She was overweight and perhaps slightly below average in her studies. Her face appeared rather coarse, and the teenage curse of acne had found its mark early. Yet no single characteristic rendered her grossly different from the rest of us.

The tougher boys rechristened Diane "Boxer," after a then renowned cartoon character. Sycophants among the boys, especially those uneasy about their own social status, presently adopted the title. Through repetition, the majority followed suit. Diane, a person, had metamorphosed into Boxer, a cartoonist hound.

For a few weeks after the name-calling began, Diane ineffectually and spiritlessly demurred. Her protestations left her vulnerable, psychologically and physically defenseless in the face of such a concerted onslaught. Occasionally, Diane complained or wept quietly; but she soon learned that her protests merely escalated the abuse.

One late fall afternoon, under the incongruously cheerful eyes of tagboard skeletons and bulletin board ghouls, Miss Torgerson called on Diane to answer a question. Other students snickered as Diane stared vacantly, lost in thought and unaware of the question. A boy disparagingly yelled, "Wake up, Boxer." She looked up with a start, asked to have the question repeated, answered it. Miss Torgerson looked uncomfortable, but she did not respond to the incident.

The campaign waged against Diane included teasing, verbal harassment, and such minor physical annoyances as poking, tripping, and pinching. Ink magically appeared on her completed work. The abuse Diane received was most intense in the absence of adults, but often it occurred in more subtle forms in their presence. Following the ineffectual period of complaint, Diane slid into anonymity. She seemed to shrink in size as she sought to disappear.

It is the greatest irony that Diane's vulnerability was her most despised characteristic. Hatred of the weak by the not-so-weak was layered shallowly beneath a thin veneer of good-natured fun. I often wondered what made students so angry about this clearly harmless girl.

Another of my fellow students, Dave, had learned to make flatulent noises by manipulating his hand under his armpit. Another student once commented that this was by far Dave's greatest accomplishment and was rewarded for the intemperate remark with a bloody nose. Dave took his repu-tation, if not his studies, seriously. He was physically mature, larger, and tougher than all of the boys and most of the girls.

While Miss Torgerson drank coffee in the teachers' lounge one day during the hectic weeks leading up to Christmas, Dave sneaked up behind Diane's desk, where she slouched, endeavoring to remain unnoticed. He generated a ripping noise that echoed through the room. He shouted to the ensuing silence, "God damn, Boxer, did you fart again?" Mocking laughter and dog barks rose up in the room.

Diane's face reddened. She rose so abruptly that Dave put up his hands as if to protect his face or square off for fisticuffs. She ran out of the room, crying and screaming unin-telligibly. Her strangled voice came out in sobs, frighteningly adult in their anguish. I had never experienced such hopeless, deeply felt grief in someone my own age.

Our treatment of Diane was literally torture. I despised myself for not intervening. I longed to have the adults in my life help me make sense of the situation and my feelings about it. I wanted some force to swoop down and fix Diane's predicament. Perhaps simple-mindedly, I hoped the primary perpetrators would be brought to justice.

My question required explanations: What made a vulnerable student such a potent magnet for peer abuse? Once students knew that the teasing was hurtful, why did they increase it in frequency and viciousness?

As the adult descendent of that sixth-grade boy, I work to make sense of events for the boy. In one sense, this is why I study bullying.

Like Dr. Hoover, many have ignored the issue, distancing themselves, not wanting to get involved. And schools have frequently encouraged such behavior by reinforcing the notion that this is a "normal" part of development and students should "mind their own business." Some children are fearful that they may become victims if they interfere.

It is necessary, therefore, to provide this silent majority with skills to support these values. They need to develop these skills and practice employing them in a school setting. This is best accomplished within the context of a school-wide program. The following activities are a few ways that teachers can encourage children to support victims. They were developed by the Wellesley College Center for Research on Women and the National Education Association. A school-wide team (parents, teachers, and administration) can discuss ways to implement these activities.

Courage By Degrees

Evaluation and Discussion

(1 Class Session)

Objectives

To evaluate the varying degrees of courage needed to respond to different teasing and bullying incidents; to discuss how the factors of popularity and age influence whether or not and how a bystander intervenes.

Preparation

Students can do this activity individually or in pairs. Each student (or pair of students) needs a pencil and piece of paper to begin.

Activity

- Pose each of the following bullying or teasing scenarios to the class. After each example, ask students to write down the degree of courage they think it would take to intervene—on a scale of 1–4, with "1" indicating the least amount of courage and "4" indicating the most. Ask students to write a one- or two-sentence rational for the degree of courage they think is required in each scenario. Progress quickly through the list.
- How much courage does it take to . . . ?

1. Tell one of your friends to stop teasing a kid you don't know very well?
2. Tell one of the popular kids to stop making fun of someone you don't know very well?
3. Tell a bully to stop picking on a kid you don't like?
4. Stick up for your best friend?
5. Step in if a kid who doesn't like you is targeted by a bully?
6. Tell a bully to stop teasing a kid who has bullied *you* in the past?
7. Tell a bully to stop picking on someone who doesn't have many friends?
8. Tell someone to stop bullying if *you* are very popular?
9. Include a new girl or boy in a game?
10. Confront a group of bullies who are pushing a kid around?
11. Confront a bully who is your age and teasing a younger kid?
12. Tell your parents or a relative about someone who is bullying you?

13. Tell your teacher about someone who is bullying you?

14. Tell your teacher about someone who is bullying another student?

15. Tell an older kid to stop saying mean things to someone your age?

16. Ignore someone who teases you while you are playing?

17. Run away from a bully?

18. Run away if you're outnumbered by a group of bullies?

19. Say something to a girl who is picking on a boy?

20. Say something to a boy who is picking on a girl?

Debriefing

After you have read all of the scenarios aloud to the class, discuss with students the different degrees of courage it takes to stand up for oneself or someone else in varying contexts. Possible questions to prompt discussion:

1. Which situation(s), in your opinion, requires the most courage of all (a "3" or a "4") to intervene? Why is it so hard to act in this case?

2. When is it easiest (a "1" or a "2") to help out someone who's being teased or bullied? How are these situations different from the others?

3. How does popularity influence courage?

4. Does age influence courage? How?

5. Does it matter where a situation takes place (e.g., in public or in private)?

6. What's the most courageous thing you've ever done or seen someone else do for another person who was being teased or bullied?

7. In the situations where it's hardest to intervene, can you think of some things that might make it easier to be courageous?

8. What is it about a bully that gives him/her so much power?

The "silent majority" needs skills and reinforcement in order to provide support for the victims of bullies.

32

HELPING THE BULLIES

Most schools provide help for bullies in a variety of ways. Bullies may be seen by school social workers, school psychologists, guidance counselors, and administrators. Their parents may be summoned to come to school to meet with principals and teachers. Parents of bullies may need professional help outside of school. In all, a great deal of time and money is spent dealing with the "bully." Some schools have attempted to provide parents with assistance. However, it is difficult to get parents involved.

Overall, the professional literature does not support direct intervention with bullies. What appears to be effective are clear-cut rules and consequences for bullying and staff development of a school-wide program.

Typically the focus is on decreasing aggressive behaviors, increasing empathy, and developing conflict resolution and social skills.

Dr. Garrity and her colleagues at the Cherry Creek School District in Colorado suggest the following goals for intervention with bullies:
- Decrease bullying and aggressive behaviors
- Replace thinking errors with correct thinking
- Develop more realistic self-concepts
- Increase empathy skills
- Improve normal reasoning abilities
- Encourage more appropriate anger expression
- Improve social problem-solving skills

Many of these are long-term goals. Some appear to be easier to change than others. However, an effort needs to be made to change this pattern of behavior. Again, this is done in conjunction with a school-wide program, not as a substitute.

Dr. Terrence Webster-Doyle, an expert on child behavior and the author of *Why Is Everybody Always Picking on Me?*, provides excellent role-playing activities for bullies:

Parents can alternate the role of the bully and the bully's alter ego. If you have more than one child, they can alternate roles and the parent can serve as a facilitator. Obviously, the activities below can be applied in the school setting in either a large or small group setting. In either home or school, the questions that follow the role-playing will generate meaningful discussions.

Here is how to do it. Read the part of the Bully (the parent and child can alternate) as well as the part of the Bully's Alter Ego (the bully's thought and feelings). The lines in italics should not be read; the Bully should act these out.

1. Really get into the part.
2. Act out the Alter Ego (what you think and feel).
3. Stop! and Think!
4. Ask for help if you need it.
5. Use the script to think up your own role-plays.

Role-play #1

Bully: (Alter Ego #1) Boy, I really feel like letting this kid have it.

He is acting like a crybaby. *Bully, get ready to punch the kid.*

STOP! THINK!

Bully: (Alter Ego #2) Yeah, but what good will it do to hit this mama's boy? He's just trying to get sympathy. *Bully unclenches his fist.*

Bully: Why are you acting like such a wimp? You are just feeling sorry for yourself.

Questions:
1. How did it feel to get angry with the kid?
2. How did it feel to almost punch him?
3. How did it feel to let the fist go?
4. How did it feel to talk to the kid?

Role-play #2

Bully: (Alter Ego # 1) I know she is better off than me. Look at those neat clothes and that super car her parents drive. I feel like giving her a hard time.

She is always showing off.

STOP! THINK!

Bully: (Alter Ego #2) Yeah, but who cares, anyhow? I don't really like that type of dress. Maybe someday I'll earn enough money to have fine clothes. Why waste my time on this? I've got better things to do. She does look great, though.

Bully: Hi Sarah, I like what you're wearing. You look great.

Questions:
1. How did it feel to get angry with Sarah?
2. How did it feel to want to give her a hard time?
3. How did it feel to let go of your hostile feeling?
4. How did it feel to give Sarah a compliment?

Role-play #3

Bully: (Alter Ego #1) I know he bumped into me on purpose. I'll show him. *Bully gets ready to punch the other person.*

STOP! THINK!

Bully: (Alter Ego #2) He apologized, said it was an accident. Look at the look on his face. He is afraid of me. *Bully relaxes.*

Bully: Okay. I accept your apology. Accidents happen. Just be more careful next time.

Questions:
   1. How did it feel to get bumped into?
   2. What memories came to mind when you got bumped?
   3. Did the apology sound sincere?
   4. What did the fear on his face tell you?
   5. How did it feel to accept his apology?

Role-play #4

Bully: (Alter Ego #1) What a stuck-up kid she is. She won't even look at me. She thinks she's too good for me.

STOP! THINK!

Bully: (Alter Ego #2) Okay, she's stuck-up. Why should I let that get to me? I'm okay. I don't need to walk around with my nose in the air.

Bully: You know, I think you've got a problem. How come you're so stuck on yourself? You know, you could have more friends if you weren't so conceited.

Questions:
   1. How did you get the thought that she was too good for you?
   2. How did it make you feel to think of her as stuck-up?
   3. What made you take your focus off of her and to see yourself as okay?
   4. How did it feel to tell her that she has a problem?
   5. Do you want to be friends with her?

Role-play #5

Bully: (Alter Ego #1) What a nerd. Look at that jerk's jacket. Full of inky pens and scraps of paper. What a brain. Maybe I'll knock his squeaky bike over.

STOP! THINK!

Bully: (Alter Ego #2) Hey, he could help me with my math. He's a real whiz at it.

Bully: Listen, maybe you could do me a favor. Maybe I could do you one in return? I'm good at working on bikes, you're good at algebra. Maybe we could trade.

Questions:

1. How did it feel to want to push the kid around—to put him down and knock over his bike?
2. What happened inside you when you stopped and thought?
3. How did you feel when you remembered he's got a sharp brain for math, your weakest subject?
4. How did it feel to express an interest in working with him instead of pushing him around?

Role-play #6

Bully: (Alter Ego #1) What a weakling. She can't even do one chin-up.

Bully: (Alter Ego #2) I guess that is not her thing. I wouldn't want to be that skinny, but I guess that is her business.

Bully: Hey, bones! Just kidding. Need help with your training? Let me give you a couple of tips. Honest! Come over here and I'll show you how to be Superwoman in no time. I'm serious! There is hope for those bony biceps.

Questions:

1. How did it feel to want to call her a weakling?
2. What thought went through your head when you went from putting her down to sympathizing with her?
3. How did it feel to kid her?
4. How did it feel to offer her help?
5. How did it feel to make the situation humorous?

These are a few examples of what can run through your child's head and what you can do to change your child's negative thinking to positive thinking. The point to remember is that although your child may think and feel like bullying someone, he doesn't have to. Children have the power to turn their thinking around. Sometimes doing it takes more strength than bullying. You can read the following to your child:

There are times when we all feel hurt, and times when we all want to strike out. But if we STOP and THINK, we can find peaceful ways to behave and still get what we want.

Talking Things Over

If you feel angry, talk to someone. Tell them how you feel. It's okay to feel! No matter what the feeling is! If your brain is full of revengeful thoughts, share them with a trusted friend. Sometimes just talking can help relieve the tension created by hurtful or fearful thoughts and feelings.

There are people around you who care and want to help you. You are not bad or wrong. But you may need to make some changes so you can feel better. It may seem tough at first, but you can do it! Millions of people who grow up in terrible situations and become bullies learn how to grow out of it. They understand that the way out of it is a new way into their own minds—a different way of looking at things and a real desire to change.

What you need to change is your behavior:

1. Interest in wanting to change
2. Energy that inspires a feeling of wanting to act
3. Commitment to carry it through
4. Awareness of what is happening
5. Skills that provide the ability to change
6. Alternatives for acting differently

Do you have these qualifications? If you are a bully, or if you are someone who has been bullied, you can change and do things that will help you. Here are a few suggestions:

1. Talk to your parents about what you feel.
2. Request a family time when you can all share your lives together.
3. Think and talk about ways you can get what you want without hurting other people.
4. Practice these ways.
5. Appreciate who you are; praise yourself for doing things you feel proud of.
6. Instead of teasing your friends and family, help them.
7. Communicate in ways that make you feel good and make others feel happy.
8. Find friends that support the positive sides of yourself.
9. Watch healthy, nonviolent television programs.
10. Play video games that make you feel creative and peaceful. Many of them are even more exciting and challenging than the violent ones.
11. Be selective in choosing movies to see.

And finally, some reflective questions for bullies to ponder:

1. Do you believe that might is right?
2. If so, who taught you this?
3. What influence does the media have on you as far as bullying is concerned?
4. Who are your heroes?
5. Are they really heroes, or could they be villains in disguise?
6. Do you believe in harsh punishment for children who disobey?
7. If you do, why?
8. Do you think that young people bully because they feel hurt?
9. Do you think that bullies act that way for the fun of it?
10. If you think so, why?
11. Do you believe that boys will be boys and that it's okay to be tough and to push people around?
12. Do you feel the pressure to conform?
13. Do you feel the pressure to compete?
14. Do you feel the pressure to be an A student?
15. To be a super athlete?
16. To get into the best college?
17. Do you think trying to be perfect (good) is harmful, a form of bullying oneself?
18. What type of bullies can you think of?
19. What are the effects of bullying individually?
20. What are the effects of bullying globally?
21. Do you think that a victim can cause bullying in some ways?
22. Are only boys bullies?
23. What are the differences between male and female bullies?

24. What makes you want to fight: For the fun of it? Being called a coward? To save face? Standing up for yourself? A special cause? Your country?

25. Do you think that bullying creates the enemy? How?

26. Do you believe that fighting solves problems?

27. Can violence bring about peace?

28. What can you do to create more peace: In your home? In your school? In your community? In the world?

29. Do you see yourself as a peacemaker? If not, why not?

30. Do you really care about changing?

31. Do you really care about helping others to change?

32. Are you willing to get help if you need it?

33. Isn't it really up to you?

QUESTIONS AND ANSWERS

Do boys bully more than girls?

The bullying tactics that boys use are more physical and observable, and therefore it appears that most bullies are boys. However, girls also bully and the tactics they use tend to be verbal—using intimidation, spreading rumors, and the like.

How pervasive is the problem?

Approximately 15 percent of schoolchildren are involved in bullying incidents. Six percent are bullies and 9 percent are victims.

Do bullies have low self-esteem?

No. Bullies have average or better self-esteem as well as friends. This is contrary to what most people think.

Do bullies do poorly in school?

Bullies perform on or above grade level throughout the elementary school years. As they continue throughout the school years, they tend to get involved in "marginal" groups and to do poorly in school.

How do victims perform academically?

Victims frequently miss school due to fear and do not perform up to their potential. School is not a safe environment and their fear leads to poor school performance.

Is the expression "once a victim, always a victim" true?

Victims can learn how to deal with bullies, but first they must learn that they can depend on adults to intervene. Once they know that, they can learn techniques to deal with bullies.

Do bullies "outgrow" their behavior?

Not only do bullies not outgrow this pattern, they appear to become parents of bullies. They tend to get involved in the criminal justice system much more so than those who are not bullies and have a difficult time in breaking the generational cycle.

What can schools do about bullying?

Schools must establish school-wide programs. This problem cannot be solved on a teacher-by-teacher basis. Everyone must be involved in a program that has clear-cut rules and consequences, staff development, and a zero tolerance for bullying.

What is the single most effective deterrent to bullying?

Adult authority. Children need to know that this is not something that they have to solve by themselves. They need to know that they can go to an adult for help and that the adult will know how to deal with the problem.

GLOSSARY

Attention deficit disorder (ADD) difficulty in concentrating and staying on task. It may or may not include hyperactivity.

Attention deficit hyperactivity disorder (ADHD) difficulty in concentrating and staying on task. Hyperactivity causes part of the attention deficit.

Bullying frequent, ongoing physical and/or verbal attacks.

Inclusion a philosophy proposing that all students with special educational needs be educated in the regular classroom.

Learning disability (LD) a term used to describe children with average intelligence who are not achieving up to potential. It is presumed to be due to central nervous system dysfunction.

Modeling the tendency for children to copy specific behaviors displayed by significant people in their environment.

Passive victims shy, emotional children who respond to bullies.

Provocative victims impulsive children who may "annoy" others, yet are not effective in defending themselves.

Punishment an event that decreases the chance that a behavior will occur.

Reinforcement an event that increases the chance that a behavior will occur.

School-wide program a program in which all staff are involved in development and implementation and which is carried out in a consistent manner throughout the school.

Social perception how you interpret social situations.

Social skills skills necessary to meet the basic demands of everyday life.

Appendix A

TYPES OF REINFORCERS

The following list of reinforcers has been modified from a list developed by Dr. R. Vance Hall of the University of Kansas. Although it is not exhaustive, it does provide parents with a good start.

Potential Reinforcers for Preschoolers

Social Reinforcers

Verbal

1. Specific praise.
2. Indirect praise (telling someone else how good they are).
3. Suggested words or phrases: "Yes." "Great." "That's right." "That's fine." "Good." "Uh-huh." "Keep going." "OK." "All right." "Pretty." "Doing better." "I like that." "Good job." "I'm pleased." "I'm proud of you." "Show us how." "You're polite." "Thank-you." "I'm glad to see you." "It makes me happy when you . . . " "I like the way you . . . " "Do that again for me."

Physical

Hugs. Kisses. Smiles. Eye contact. Tickle. Wink. Handshake. Touch. Toss into the air or whirl around. Piggyback ride. Pat on the back. Chuckling/cheering. Jumping up and down. Tweaking nose.

Material Reinforcers

Toys/balloons. Books/puzzles/magazines. Snacks of favorite food. Pennies for bank.

Activity Reinforcers

Trip to park, zoo, library (any special outing). Going to work with Dad or Mom. Play with friends. Listening to stories or songs/singing songs. Play on swing set or in sandbox. Spending the night with Grandma/Grandpa or favorite adult. Opportunity to feed pet. Rocking. Playing a game/playing catch with parent/having a friend over to play or eat. Finger play. Take a picture of how good they are while they are (a) sitting on a potty, (b) displaying good table manners, (c) going to bed. Talking into a tape recorder/listening to records. Going out for a meal, snack, or movie. Playing with dough or clay. Finger painting/coloring. Blowing bubbles. Helping Mom or Dad. Longer time in bathtub or not having to take a bath (also bubble bath). Ride in a car or on a bicycle with adult/riding tricycle. Extended bedtime—skip nap. Watching TV. Going outside (day or night). Help hold baby/help give baby a bath. Swimming/being pulled in a wagon/swinging. Carry purse or attaché case for adult. Display of artwork. Playing with toys. Using telephone to tell of success. Special ride on escalator or elevator. Helping cook a meal or choosing the menu. Help water grass, flowers, or plant a garden. Camping out in the backyard.

Token Reinforcers

Stars on a chart, backed by material and activity reinforcers listed above.

Potential Reinforcers for Elementary Children (Ages 5–11) at Home

Social Reinforcers

Verbal

1. Specific praise.
2. Indirect praise (telling someone else about what they did or accomplished).
3. Suggested words and phrases: "Yes." "OK!" "Neat." "Good." "Great." "Delightful." "Brilliant." "Swell." "Fine answer." "That's right." "Beautiful." "Exciting." "Positively." "Go ahead." "Yeah." "All right." "Correct." "Marvelous." "Nifty." "Excellent." "Cool." "Outstanding." "Go on." "Good response." "Wonderful job." "Fantastic." "Absolutely." "Of course!" "Fabulous." "That's clever." "I'm pleased." "Thank-you." "I'm glad you're here." "It makes me happy when you . . . " "You perform well . . . " "I'm so proud of you for . . . " "You do so well at . . . " "We think a lot of you when . . . " "That puts you tops on our list." "That shows a great deal of work." "That's a nice expression." "That's interesting." "That's very thoughtful." "Show me how to do that." "You're doing better." "I like that." "This is the best yet." "You were polite to . . . " "No one could have done it better." "Let's put this somewhere special." "Show this to your father/mother."

Physical

Hugs/squeeze. Kisses. Handshake. Wink. "OK" gesture with thumb. Pat on the back. A teasing gesture. Eye contact.

Material Reinforcers

Toys. Tricycle. Bicycle. Balls, jump ropes, other playground equipment. Pets. Books. Games. Puzzles. Food. Own bedroom. Clothing. Musical instruments. Skates/skateboard.

Records. Own TV-radio-stereo. Personal items such as hair dryer, own telephone. Choice of seat in room. Special pencil or pen.

Activity Reinforcers

Playing game with parent. Spending time with parent. Special outing. Play with friends. Reading or being read to. Overnight with relative or friend. Decorating room or home for special event. Helping parent (cook, work in yard, sew, or construct something). Feed the baby. Extended bedtime. Shopping. Eating out. Plan a day's activities. Watching TV or listening to records. Freedom from chores. Using the telephone. Planting a garden. Taking special lessons (such as music, athletic, art). Public display of work. Party for friends. Going to hamburger stand.

Token Reinforcers
(backed by reinforcers listed above)

Stars on a chart. Points, chips. Allowance. Own bank account.

Potential Reinforcers for Middle School Youths
(Ages 12–14) at Home

Social Reinforcers

Verbal

1. Specific praise.
2. Kidding and joking.
3. Suggested words or phrases: "Neat." "Fantastic." "Wow." "Super." "Great." "Nice." "On a scale of 1 to 10, you are an 11!" "It is a pleasure having you as a . . . (son or daughter)." "I'm proud of you." "I like your attitude (behavior)." "That was very thoughful." "You just made my life easier." "You are a lot of help." "You do so well at . . ." It pleases me when you . . . " "I like that outfit." "That's so-o-o good." "Show us how to do that." "That's better."

Physical

Smiles. Eye contact. Physical contact (only if adolescent approves). Winks.

Material Reinforcers

Favorite meal. Snack. Clothes. Books and magazines. Own phone-TV-radio. Stereo. Tapes. CDs. Electric razor. Hair dryer. Own room. Gift certificate. Guitar or other musical instruments. Money. Sports equipment. Hobby items. Own pet.

Activity Reinforcers

Participate in activities with friends. Special lessons (such as music, sports, modeling, art). Roller skating. Additional time on telephone. Playing stereo. Choosing own bedtime. Extended curfew. Staying up late. Staying overnight with friends. Time off from assigned chores. Opportunity to earn money. TV privileges. Being chairperson of a family meeting. Decorating own room. Camping out. Summer camp. Expensive haircut. Trip to amusement park. Sleeping late. Discussion with parents. School activities. Party for friends. Taking a friend out for a pizza. Shopping trip (clothes). Ski trip. Bowling. Sporting events. Time with parents alone (apart from younger brothers and sisters).

Token Reinforcers

Points (backed by a reinforcer above). Money.

Potential Reinforcers for Senior High Youths (Ages 15–18) at Home

Social Reinforcers

Verbal

1. Specific praise.
2. Kidding and joking.
3. Indirect praise (telling someone else about what they did or accomplished).

4. Suggested words or phrases: "Swell." "All right." "Super." "Great." "Bravo." "Well done." "Commendable." "Delightful." "Excellent." "Likable." "Terrific." "How true." "Good job." "That's clever." "I'm pleased." "I'm glad you're here." "That's a prize of a job." "It makes me happy when you . . . " "Lookin' good." "Yeah." "How beautiful." "Well thought out." "You are very sincere." "That shows thought." "This is the best yet." "Now you're really trying." "You have a good attitude." "Keep up the good work." "Your room looks so neat." "Whatever you decide is okay." "That was a good suggestion." "What is your opinion." "What would you suggest?"

Physical

Smiles. Eye contact. Nods. Physical contact (only if adolescent approves).

Material Reinforcers

Books. Pets. Playing cards. Games. Musical instruments. CDs. Tapes. Sports equipment. Tools to work on car or motorcycle. Computer, CD player, TV. Own telephone. Clothes. Electrical equipment (shaver, hair dryer, makeup mirror). Craft kits. Favorite foods. Car keys. Money.

Activity Reinforcers

Leading family groups. Exempting a duty or assigned tasks. Cooking. Working on a car or cycle. Listening to TV, stereo, tapes. Talking on the telephone. Free time with peer group. Special outing (parent pays) such as, musical group, sporting event, bowling, roller/ice skating, movie. Remodeling, redecorating room. Shopping trip. Friend overnight or staying with friend.

Token Reinforcers

Points (appropriate for some 14 to 15 year olds, backed by material and/or activity reinforcers). Money.

The Reinforcement Questionnaire that follows is helpful with selecting reinforcers.

REINFORCEMENT QUESTIONNAIRE

Name: _____ Date: _____

School: _____ Age: _____

Filled out by: _____

1. The things I like to do most after school are
_____

2. If I had $10, I'd
_____

3. My favorite TV programs are
_____

4. My favorite game at school is
_____

5. My best friends are
_____

6. My favorite time of day is
_____

   because
_____

7. My favorite toys are
_____

8. My favorite records or tapes are
_____

9. My favorite subject at school is
_____

10. I like to read books about
_____

11. The places I'd like to go in town are
_____

12. My favorite foods are
_____

13. My favorite inside activities are

_____

14. My favorite outside activities are

_____

15. My hobbies are

_____

16. My favorite animals are

_____

17. The three things I like to do most are

_____

_____

_____

18. The three things I like to do least are

_____

_____

_____

Appendix B

~~~~~~

RESOURCES FOR PARENTS

- Due to the fact that such a high percentage of victims are children who are classified as learning disabled and/or attention deficit disorder, the following books would be beneficial:

McNamara, B. E. and Francine J. McNamara (1993). *Keys To Parenting a Child with Attention Deficit Disorder.* Hauppauge, NY: Barron's Educational Series, Inc.

McNamara, B. E. and Francine J. McNamara (1995). *Keys to Parenting a Child with a Learning Disability.* Hauppauge, NY: Barron's Educational Series, Inc.

- For all parents, but perhaps especially for parents of bullies, effective parenting techniques are critical. The following two books, available from Research Press, Department 971, P.O. Box 9177, Champaign, Illinois, are excellent:

Becker, W. (1971) *Parents are Teachers.*

Patterson, G. (1976) *Living with Children.*

Appendix C

RESOURCES
FOR CHILDREN

One of the major resources for children are books that portray incidents of bullying and effective ways to resolve the conflict. Despite the number of good books on the topic, it is surprising to find that quite a few employ ineffective techniques. There are some that continue to advocate physical aggression. Others have unrealistic expectations for change, and others provide no help whatsoever. A word of caution: Review the books before reading them with your child (a good idea for any book) and make sure that they follow the basic guidelines for dealing with this issue.

The following are a sampling of books appropriate for children:

Amos (1993). *Bully*. New York: Benchmark.

Anders, E. (1995). *Jody and the Bully*. New York: Grosset & Dunlap.

Bosh, C.W. (1988). *Bully on the Bus*. Seattle, WA: Parenting Press

Brown, M. (1990). *Arthur's April Fool*. Boston: Little Brown & Co.

Carlson, N. (1983). *Loudmouth George and the Sixth Grade Bully*. New York: Puffin Books.

Carrick, C. (1983). *What a Wimp.* New York: Clarion Books.

Craring, E. (1983). *My Name Is Not Dummy.* Seattle, WA: Parenting Press.

Duffey, B. (1993). *How to Be Cool in the Third Grade.* New York: Viking.

Griffe, T. (1991). *Bully For You.* New York: Child Play.

Howe, J. (1996). *Pinky and Rex the Bully.* New York: Aladdin Paperbacks.

Lowenstein, C. (1994). *Fair Play.* New York: W. H. Freeman.

Petty, K. and C. Firmin. (1991). *Being Bullied.* Hauppauge, NY: Barron's Educational Series, Inc.

Shyston, J. (1995). *No Biting, Horrible Crocodile!* New York: Golden Books.

Stein, M. (1992). *How to Survive Fifth Grade.* Mahwah, NJ: Troll Associates.

Susanne, J. (1996). *Don't Talk To Brian.* New York: Bantam Books.

Webster-Doyle, T. (1991). *Why Is Everybody Always Picking on Me? A Guide to Handling Bullies for Young People.* Middlebury, VT: Atrium Society.

Appendix D

RESOURCES FOR SCHOOLS

T he most effective intervention for schools is the development and implementation of a school-wide program. *Bully-Proofing Your School—A Comprehensive Approach For Elementary Schools*, written by Carla Garrity, Ph.D., Kathryn Jens, Ph.D., William Porter, Ph.D., Nancy Sager, and Cam Short-Camilli, C.S.W., is superb. It is thorough, provides a wealth of practical information, and contains resources for school personnel, parents, and children. It is published by Sopris West, 1140 Boston Avenue, Longmont, Colorado 80501.

Bullying At School by Dr. Daniel Olweus (Blackwell Publishers, Inc., 238 Main Street, Cambridge, Massachusetts 02142) is considered to be the definitive work on bullying. School districts considering a program to deal with bullying should consider this excellent, thoroughly researched book.

The Wellesley College Center for Research on Women in conjunction with the National Education Association developed a guide to dealing with bullies in schools. It provides educators with specific instructional activities and also includes an excellent section on resources. It is available from Wellesley College's Publications Department, 106 Central Street, Wellesley, Massachusetts 02181-8259.

Resources that are particularly useful for schools in their effort to evaluate the effectiveness of a school-wide program include:

Olweus, D. (1991). *Bully/Victim Problems Among School Children.*

Basic facts and effects of a school-based intervention program are found in D. Peppler and K. Rubin (Eds.), *The Development and Treatment of Childhood Aggression.* Hillsdale, NJ: Erlbaum.

Olweus, D. (1991). *Bullying Among School Children, Intervention and Prevention.* In R. D. Peters, R. J. McMahan, and V. L. Quincy (Eds)., *Aggression and Violence Through The Life Span.*

Social Skills Programs

The following are a list of social skills training programs that can be implemented in school settings.

ASSET: A Social Skills Program for Adolescents with Learning Disabilities (Research Press). A social skills program based on instruction in learning strategies.

DUSO (Developing Understanding of Self and Others (American Guidance Services). Activities and kits to stimulate social and emotional development in children in grades K–4.

Getting Along with Others (Research Press). Teaching students skills for being in group activities.

Skill Streaming the Adolescent: A Structural Learning Approach to Teaching Prosocial Skills (Research Press). Activities for developing social skills in adolescents.

Skill Streaming the Elementary School Child: A Guide for Teaching Prosocial Skills (Research Press). Activities for developing social skills in elementary school children.

Social Skill Instruction for Daily Living (American Guidance Services). Activities for adolescents with learning disabilities.

Social Skills Intervention (American Guidance Services). A social skills program for students with learning disabilities.

The Social Skills Curriculum (American Guidance Services). A curriculum for teaching social skills.

TAD (Toward Affective Development) (American Guidance Services). Group activities, lessons, and materials to stimulate psychological and affective development for students in grades 3 through 6.

The Walker Social Skills Curriculum: The Accepts Program (PRO-ED). Activities for developing social skills within the school.

INDEX